# HOW TO BUILD A SECURED FINANCIAL FUTURE

Sunday Adelaja

Sunday Adelaja
**HOW TO BUILD A SECURED FINANCIAL FUTURE**
©2017 Sunday Adelaja
ISBN 978-1-908040-36-7


Copyright © Golden Pen Limited
Milton Keynes, United Kingdom. All rights reserved
www.goldenpenpublishing.com

Cover design by Alexander Bondaruk
Interior design by Olena Kotelnykova

# TABLE OF CONTENTS

# INTRODUCTION

Most people at some point in their lives have experienced a financial crisis, debt or poverty. Income levels on the other hand across the world have gone up. Even the poorest continent in the world is experiencing an emerging middle class as measured by their income levels. Yet people continue to have difficulties in retaining this money. These are people who have mastered their craft, overcome great difficulties and yet when it comes to money they are unable to attain financial freedom.

People are still trapped in the webs they have woven around their lives. They are either living for survival or for the applause of others. You may love your job and find fulfillment and purpose in it, but the money you make from it is not enough, you cannot meet the growing needs of your family. You have a well paying job but you are constantly in debt or living from paycheck to paycheck. You still long in the deep recesses of your heart to do things that are significant, that will make a difference in the world but you can't. You cannot let go of your job, your expenses won't let you.

If you are not living for things of eternal value beyond yourself and your family, you are not alive. You are trapped in meaningless activity. The world system is engineered to keep you trapped. In most countries of the world, over 90% of the country's wealth and power is in the hands of less than 3% of the population. The remaining 97% of the population is caught up in the trap of salary or vanities. The way the system is set up, people mistakenly assume that because they earn a salary, they are paying themselves. It is common to hear people brag about how much salary they are paid.

The consumer culture in the world is part of the system. The world constantly bombards with things you need to spend money on. Spend money to buy a big car; for status. Spend money on the best clothes; because you deserve the best. Products are packaged in attractive ways to appeal to your eyes. Advertisements, both obvious ones and the subtle ones, are constantly pushing you to spend money, enticing you with your own desires. In this way the system ensures, no matter how much more you keep making you cannot satisfy all you want. You are forced to work even harder. The need for a better paying job is constant because with time your needs increase.

This book will change how you view the world, money and your passion. These three things are not independent of each other; they are connected and are core to your financial freedom. I will open your eyes to how they are connected and how that can make a difference to your future. *How to build a secured financial future* was written to challenge and change your beliefs about money, savings and investments and their connection to your current world and your future. I wanted to set others free who keep experiencing the same cycle, same frustration around money. No matter how much you earn money is never enough? You have to work more hours doing things you don't necessarily enjoy to make ends meet. If you yearn for more than this rat race but do not know how to free yourself from the limitations of your salary to doing what you love, this book is for you. If you can learn to properly align these three things; Your Money, Your Passion and The World, we would have achieved our objective. You will learn how to control and manage your money towards your passion. I will show you how to succeed in making savings and then investments and the secret to succeeding at paying yourself and building your future, where you have only failed in the past.

You have a call to greatness which is your passion. You have to live beyond survival or vanity. To get back your time and focus on your calling, you have to set yourself free from the enslavement of the world system. To outsmart this system and secure your financial future, you have to pay yourself.

# CHAPTER 1

# THE TRAP OF THE WORLD SYSTEM

**Everything that belongs to the world......
what the sinful self desires, what people
see and want, and everything in this world
that people are so proud of.......none of this
comes from the Father; it all comes from the
world.**

*(1 John 2:16 Good News Bible)*

*Everything that is in the world including the
system that runs it does not belong to God. As a
result it is an oppressive system that enslaves,
traps and destroys people. You need to understand
it and how it works before setting yourself free
from the grip of it.*

A study by Princeton University found that income
did not contribute to the emotional well-being of an
individual above a household income of $75,000 per year
in the United States of America. The study did confirm
the contribution of higher income to improving individuals' satisfaction with their lives. For even among those
who were already well off but only up to a point[1]. Advertising on the other hand is geared to stir up emotions
that cause discontentment with one's life. They create in

you the need for the advertised product with the promise that the product will bring about satisfaction. Every time you watch an advert, you experience emotions of sadness, grief or elation.

Go to several countries in the world. Turn on the TV or radio and listen to the adverts. I believe you will quickly notice similarities in the messages being passed on by these adverts across the countries. The first most prevalent message passed on, whether through formalized advertising or word on the street, is that your worth is in how you look and the things you possess. The second message that is uniform across cultures is that the more money you make the more successful you are. Thirdly, the more famous you are, the more attention you receive. Other additional themes that you will pick up within the adverts are just as twisted. If you have money, there are no consequences to negative actions. Another message, only unhappy, stingy mean old people delay their pleasure, you deserve to have yours now.

## A CULTURE DRIVEN BY CONSUMERISM

Globalization has led to a culture driven by consumerism. In this culture, an individual's value is defined by material symbols. The pressure is tremendous to conform to uniform images of the good life. Japan, the former Soviet countries, Africa and the BRIC[2] countries are heavily influenced by consumer culture in western countries. The latent qualities that come with such a culture have become pervasive in these countries. Japan, for example, is a big consumer of luxury brands as a result of their value for high priced quality material goods. Increasingly a higher proportion of their income is spent on leisure and luxury while the portion spent on basic necessities has reduced. Indians save a quarter of their incomes in cash accounts and this is largely used up during family ceremonies. However an emerging middle class in India have a high appetite for branded goods advertised through television. The media paints an illusion of the lifestyles of the rich and famous. In Africa, cars, clothing and buildings are important social status symbols. The uniformity of the increasing material desires across continents points to a common driver.

To illustrate this, let me tell you the story of my friend, Raj. He grew up in an average home, where his parents would hardly spend any money on non basic items. Despite their low incomes they succeeded in building investment income through rental houses and in taking him and his siblings through good schools. Raj on the other hand, despite earning more money than his parents would ever hope to earn, has no savings, no investments and relies solely on his salary. His house is filled with all the latest electronic gadgets, and trendiest furnitures. The people who know him and his family would say they live well, in an affluent neighborhood, having good cars and plush home. They are not in debt; he pays off credit card payments on time. He saves for his family's annual vacation, and he puts aside some money monthly for his retirement. He is better educated than his parents; in fact he works in the field of engineering. He earns much more than the minimum wage and despite wanting to save more, he is constantly finding himself with just enough money at the end of the month to cover his expenses. He is not willing according to him to 'live below a certain lifestyle.' My friend believes he has worked hard for the life he has. He rewards himself by living in one of the best homes, driving the best cars and exposing his family to the best vacation spots. Things he never had growing up. He is living the American dream. Does Raj's story sound familiar? Does it remind you of anyone you know maybe yourself? If Raj continues with his current lifestyle he will never pursue his calling. It may not seem so, but Raj is a slave to his salary. He can never afford to leave his job to pursue what he desires unless he determines to change his life. There is more to life than material pleasures. Raj's life has no impact on things of eternal value, does yours?

A system is defined as *a whole plan or scheme consisting of many parts connected in such a manner as to create a chain of mutual dependencies*[3]. The world system is therefore a scheme put in place that creates patterns of behavior, a culture and a civilization that produces similar results among the vast majority of the population. It works for the benefit of the elite few in the population while the majority is enslaved by it. The world system is an ordered system which is governed from behind the scenes by a ruler, Satan. The bible refers to him as the god of this world[4].

Edward L Bernays considered the father of public relations, in his book *Propaganda, the public mind in the making* writes:

> *'The conscious and intelligent manipulation of the organized habits and opinions of the masses is an important element in democratic society. Those who manipulate this unseen mechanism of society constitute an invisible government which is the true*

*ruling power of our country....We are governed,
our minds are molded, our tastes formed, our ideas
suggested, largely by men we have never heard of.
This is the logical result of the way in which our
democratic society is organized....'*

Bernays point is that an invisible 'government' has the power to shape values and response of the people by engineering their thoughts and opinions and therefore their habits and culture.

Advertisers are said to prod the unconscious mind into spending by using images. Vance Packard, journalist and author of *Hidden Persuaders* describes what his book is about.

*"It's about large scale efforts being made, often
with impressive success, to channel our unthinking
habits, our purchasing decisions and our thought
processes by use of insights gained from psychi-
atry and social sciences. Typically these efforts
take place beneath our level of awareness; so that
the appeals which move us are often, in a sense,
hidden. The result is that many of us are being
influenced and manipulated far more than we
realize, in the patterns of our everyday life."*

Specific tactics were used by experts in the late fifties when this book was written to affect buying habits of Americans. A classic example is in the influence of impulse buying habits in women by adverts and shop displays. This is as true today as it was in 1957 when he wrote these words. Perhaps even more true given the vast influence of television, the internet and particularly social media. My friend walked into a mall intending to shop for her household needs. By the time she left the store she had bought clothes, shoes, candy and useless knickknacks she did not intend to buy. Has this ever happened to you? You exceeded your budget, if you had any multiple times over. You run into a store to grab some milk and as you were checking out, you also bought candy and snacks displayed attractively at the checkout point. The advertising industry and thus the corporations that pay them, get people to spend money on things they can't afford and don't need to fuel their profits.

Companies are competing for your money. Most of these companies are owned by the 3% or less who control a nation. As these companies make money from the money you spend buying their goods or services, these wealthy keep getting wealthier. Even if your income continues to go up, the list of your expenses also increases because your standard of living goes up. You expand the list of the people you pay; from mortgage companies, credit card companies, petrol station owners, landlords, supermarkets, beauty shops, clothing stores, hotels, schools, hospitals, airlines and so on. The more your expenses increase the harder you need to work to maintain your lifestyle and the more dependent you become on your job. At this point you are trapped, enslaved by the world system. You are dependent on your salary and cannot leave your job to pursue your call or grow in your calling. This is the trap of the world system.

Even though my friend, Raj, is skilled at what he does and earns upwards of $200,000 a year, other people are the main beneficiaries of his income not Raj. He drives a luxurious car he bought at more than $50,000 from a top vehicle manufacturer, and lives in an affluent neighborhood at a house he bought on a 30 year mortgage. He has refinanced his mortgage once to clear credit card bills and pay for the purchase of another car for his wife. His kids attend the best private schools and he takes his family on annual vacations overseas, sometimes paid for through one of his credit cards. He has an upper middle class lifestyle and considers himself comfortable financially. He is constantly improving himself, studying and working harder. He has moved jobs a few times in his fifteen year career earning more in salary and perks each time. He has built a good life for his family and would consider this his achievement. Raj does not consider himself financially dependent or poor. The family's comfort has him trapped. He is completely dependent on his salary. He can never afford to lose his salary but the sad thing is that he doesn't see he's trapped.

This trap enslaves, people end up spending their lives, living for food, shelter and clothing. At best they are caught in the bondage of vanities, constantly chasing illusions. They pursue the dreams that they have been fed, to live large, own houses, material things and have status. By the time you finish reading this book your eyes will open to the deception and I will show you how to set yourself free from this vicious cycle. This book contains practical steps to turn your life around. I only ask you to apply the principles contained here so that you can set yourself free from frivolity and live a life of significance. You may need to take notes or underline parts of this book that speak to you and be deliberate about applying what you learn to change your life and start living for the

Kingdom of God.

The Bible describes the world; *cosmos* as consisting of the following; the pride of life, the lust of the flesh and the lust of the eyes[5]. I will explain these things further on in the book, but these are the tools the devil uses to entrap you into his system. He uses your own corrupt wants, lusts and your own desire to be esteemed and be accepted; the pride of life. The pride of life refers to taking your value from the things around you. Your desire for titles and reputation and to have a standing in society when not checked leads to the pride of life. These desires stem from how you view the world, your perspective and the beliefs you hold about the world. If you believe that the rich man is the most powerful being on earth, then your ultimate goal in life from your experience and environment will be to become rich. Your pursuit of money at all cost will consume you because of the big man image you have in your head. This desire to be rich is what the world system will use to entrap you, because you are seeking to get riches to gain an identity from it. Raj grew up in a humble home, his parents didn't have much money and many times he had to forgo what he desired because there was no money for it. Other children particularly in high school would be dropped off to school in nice cars and these kids would make fun of him because he had to take the public bus to school. He made up his mind that he would work hard and chose a path that would make him as much money as he wanted. He would never again have to do without what he wanted. No one would look down on him because of the clothes he wore or because he looked poor. As you can see Raj "made it". His upbringing influenced his ambition to make money and the money has become part of his identity. No wonder he lives the way he does. How many of you are same way? You determined that you would get a good job and prove yourself to your friends or relatives with the money you have acquired. Are you happy? Does making the money at the expense of your calling make you content? Fulfilled? Only you can answer these. But if you are reading this book, it would seem that you want more. That you want your life to impact generations, to live for the things God put you here for.

## A STRONG DESIRE TO MAKE IT

A lot of people particularly in developing countries like my country, Nigeria, have a very strong desire to make it. This is because of the environment of poverty within which they have been raised. They push themselves and work hard to make money and become wealthy. This drive to survive ends up being the very tool the devil uses to entrap them into the world system, because they want to make money by all means. In large cities within Africa, the young people attend universities to pursue courses that are guaranteed to give them a good salary. A few years back the desire was to be an engineer or lawyer or doctor because you could buy a house in a good neighborhood and drive a good car with the salary you made. Now a lot of young Africans desire to be entrepreneurs or musicians because that is what will make them a lot of money. As soon as they get an income, they have to buy a good car and move to an affluent neighborhood. They dedicate even more hours to working hard and make as much money as they can, as fast as possible. On the sad extreme, every week law enforcement officials in Singapore, Taiwan and China imprison Nigerian citizens trying to smuggle drugs into these countries. Despite the high rates of imprisonment and the news being in the media, hundreds of other Nigerians prepare to make similar journeys from Nigeria to Asia and other parts of the world. Parts of my country are well known because the drug traffickers from these areas live such flashy lifestyles and the young people idolize them. Even the threat of prison does not deter these young men from trying to make quick money. These people have given Nigerians a bad name in the world. We begin to worship money when we are driven by it. The bible calls this exaltation of money the worship of mammon, the false god of money. This system captivates them and they sell themselves into it and they cannot walk out.

In developed countries, Hollywood movies and the depiction of the American dream cause men to believe that is all their life is for. It informs their desires, their motives and therefore their habits. They are very diligent at their jobs, to be able to attain this American dream. Like my friend Raj, once they have attained this dream, they believe they have it made. Many famous and wealthy personalities, musicians, actors, TV hosts discovered only emptiness once they attained the wealth they desired and had beautiful spouses, beautiful homes and impressive cars. Incidences of famous celebrated men and women committing suicide or overdosing on drugs are not uncommon in our world today. Recently, world celebrated comedian Robin Williams was found in his room hanging from a belt. He was a wealthy and highly acclaimed actor yet for years he lived under the shadow of depression. Other celebrities at the top of their craft were addicted to drugs including prescription medicine and died as a result of these drugs. In 2009 the world received with shock the news that the 'King of Pop, Michael Jackson had died as a result of an overdose of prescription drugs. Former Nirvana front singer, Kurt Cobain died in 2000 as a result of a drug overdose. He was highly celebrated and had fans from around the world. He left behind millions of dollars in properties and other riches. If you pursue the illusion of the American dream that the world system shows you, you end up with just vanities and nothing to show for your life!

*Until you begin to see life differently, worldly desires will keep running you.*

An encounter with the Lord Jesus Christ transformed the twelve disciples, well eleven when you exclude Judas, into great apostles who were pursuing God because He changed their world view. Jesus called these men to follow Him and they were willing to follow Him and serve Him wholeheartedly. We remember Peter today because he was free to follow Jesus and do the work of an apostle with great boldness. He stood before kings and spoke about Jesus. John, Luke and Mathew published accounts of the life of Jesus and spread the gospel among the Jews. These disciples turned the world upside down and had such an impact on the world that we still remember them today, 2,000 years after their death. These men who became Jesus' disciples are remembered even today, because they were free to work for God, they left everything else they were doing. They were not trapped by any system. For a man to escape the trap of the world system, he has to change his perspective on life. If you free yourself from the trap of the world system you can serve God in your calling and change the world.

## THE DANGERS OF BEING TRAPPED

Let me tell you the story of a different friend, Thomas. Like Raj, he was earning a good income. He was providing for his family a comfortable middle class lifestyle. He kept working hard at his job and kept earning more money, which like Raj, was taken up by his comfortable living. Thomas' job came with a lot of pressure and constant travels. During one of his travels, in his hotel, he happened to lose an important work document which cost him the client contract. This put him under immense scrutiny at work that threatened his job. It is in this period that Thomas with the help of his wife began to evaluate his life and realized that he could not survive for more than three months without his job. All his comfort was just an illusion, it is his salary that was providing for their lifestyle and if it was taken away, the comfort would also go. This has been a wakeup call; Thomas has sacrificed himself all this while for his family's upkeep. Thomas was lucky to experience this shock since it has led to a significant shift in how he lives his life. You may never experience such a situation. But if you do not change how you live your life you will wake up at the end of your life and realize you have spent all your life pursuing things that do not matter. You do not have to be jolted out of your comfort zone. Make the decision to pursue your calling. Discover and pursue your God-given purpose. You don't have to wait until you have all the money, fame and relationships in the world to realize that it does not satisfy. The pursuit of wealth is not what our time here on earth is for. We are put here on earth to worship God and serve Him with our gifts and talents. Through our individual purpose, we are to advance the kingdom of God on the earth. We can be rich, in fact Christians should be rich, but the reason is to bring about heaven and God's righteousness on earth. I tackled more on how and why Christians should be rich in my book, Money won't make you rich. We can learn from the world around us and the examples of those who went before us. The rich man went to Jesus because he was seeking for something more, even though he had great possessions[6].

Is seeking first the Kingdom of God realistic? It seems easier said than done, doesn't it? After all we have bills to pay, children to educate, a spouse to provide for or families to look after. How can you realistically expect me to seek first the kingdom of God? You ask. That is why it is important to escape the trap of the world system and begin to live for God and his Kingdom, to advance His agenda on the earth. We are answerable to God for what we do while here on earth. We will give an account to God in the end for what we did on earth. This book is meant to show you how to set yourself free to pursue the kingdom of God first, read on.

## THE SNARES OF THE SYSTEM

The world system also uses things with no eternal value to get people trapped. People like you or Raj and Thomas are caught chasing dreams, illusions and trivialities created for them. These things lie to them that they will find meaning and fulfillment in keeping them. 'Successful people' as defined by the media; people with a lot of money and fame are constantly held up on our TV screens as role models. We are made to think that unless we are like those people we are not successful. This way we are programmed to think that if we look a certain way, dress in luxurious items, own vast and expansive properties that we have made it, we have become accomplished in life. Let's review some snares of the system that most of us had been trapped into.

## 1. PROSPERITY GOSPEL

Among Christians, the prosperity gospel has further propagated the pursuit of the unimportant, it has exalted the pastors who own private jets, custom made vehicles and such trivialities as the symbols of a blessed life. Jesus equated those not doing the will of God as those building houses with a foundation of sand and when the storms come, those houses are swept away because sand cannot stand the test of time[7]. Many Christians around the world are living for money and not for God. I am friends with a number of pastors around the world. I am also a pastor. Every Sunday these pastors get a lot of requests for prayer. Guess what is the most common prayer request for these Christians? Money! They want to breakthrough in their businesses and to get good jobs. A friend told me of how he would pray every day and fast when he didn't have a job. He would attend prayer meetings and fellowship meetings in addition to searching for a job. As soon as he got a job, he stopped praying. He only opens his bible during Sunday service. He is happy that even though he doesn't enjoy his job, he is paid enough to afford a good car and live in a nice location. He doesn't know his purpose but he is not too bothered by this since he has a good job. According to him having a good job is a sign of God's blessing which is enough. Are you living a similar life?

## 2. THE WORLD SYSTEM USES GOOD THINGS LIKE MARRIAGE AND CHILDREN, TO ENTRAP US

Once we marry, we have responsibilities that require money. We have children and our expenses increase a lot more. We need healthcare, school fees, food and entertainment for these children. We have to pay minders, nannies or day care centers, school fees and college tuition for them. All these things require money and so we cannot afford to be without a job or an income. In countries like the United States, one cannot live without money, because the demands and expenses are so much. If you go without an income for a short while only, you will fail to pay your bills and can easily become homeless. The more the expenses, the more our need for a well paying job to match these expenses. People keep mortgaging their time for higher and higher salaries while their expenses keep rising and rising to no end. This is the rat race, forever running but never going anywhere. Their expenses cannot allow them to leave their jobs and they have to work harder and harder, study more, become more specialized to earn more money to meet these needs. Most people are not thinking about their purpose and even if they were, they cannot pursue purpose because their responsibilities and expenses wouldn't let them.

## 3. THE EDUCATION SYSTEM IS PART OF THE PROBLEM

The education system that is currently used in most of the world was designed for a different age. In the early 1800s, during the industrial revolution, the demand was for people to work in assembly lines and factories to produce a common product. This societal demand spawned a system of education based on the Prussian model that educated students in classes according to their age. They all moved at the same pace with each getting the same amount of information per year. This model would churn out workers needed in these factories and assembly lines. It was partly responsible for the success of the Industrial revolution in early adoption countries like Germany. This education model evolved over a period of 100 years and was exported to the rest of the world through colonialism. From the early 1900s, the model has remained the same and is still geared to produce workers, people programmed to think uniformly, to take instructions without questions and produce a certain predetermined end result. It programs us to want to give our time in exchange for a salary, to think of work only in terms of a job. It causes us to only think within the confines of status quo; what is accepted in society, what has been done and is being done. We do not question how things are or have been over time. We easily accept things as being part of our culture. This affects even organizations that only think of doing things the same way. If they come up with something, they compare with similar organizations to see whether it has been done before.

## 4. The dominant culture that celebrates achievements

The culture we are part of celebrates achievements, particularly achievements that come with great financial rewards. Top athletes earning lots of money from their games, earn even more from endorsement contracts from different companies. Advertisers and companies parade them and use them to sell products. They know the culture has esteemed these athletes so much, everybody wants to be like them. Advertisers have used campaigns like *"BE LIKE MIKE"* to sell us shoes and other products because they knew people wanted to be like the legendary American basketball player Michael Jordan. Even entrepreneurs who have made billions within 5 to 10 years are constantly in the news. We are always told how much they are worth and the size of the companies they have built. They have superstar status around the world. They are ranked in world famous magazines such as Forbes in order of their wealth; the one with the highest net worth is ranked first. As a result, many people are living for achievements, to make money so that they too can be celebrated.

Over a 30 year period, Mobutu Sese Seko Kuku Ngbenda Wa Za Banga reigned as the ruler of the Democratic Republic of Congo, then known as Zaire, in Africa. During that period he amassed a personal fortune estimated between $1Billion and $5 Billion dollars[8]. He had plush palatial residences in Paris, Lausanne in Switzerland. He loved the comforts of life. He is said to have enjoyed pink champagne and even had fresh cakes flown in from Paris for his consumption. All this wealth was illicitly acquired from the nation, one of the poorest in the world. These stories are common in the developing countries; politicians command a lot of power and wealth, because of rampant corruption. In fact the quickest way to become wealthy in most African countries is to become a politician. They are the *'Big Men'* in those societies. This culture of celebrating 'big men' is the theme of a similarly named documentary produced by actor Brad Pitt about the discovery of oil in Ghana. It shows how the 'Big Man' is exalted in that society and in Nigeria and how much the push to be a 'big man' drives the people. It becomes the ambition of the people, their sole *raison d'être*( reason for being). Tales like these drive the masses to want to be big, to achieve status within society and to be celebrated by society. They spend their lives pursuing money, some through honest and others through dishonest means. Money is their reason for living. They are willing to pursue money at whatever cost and many acquire it through corrupt dealings. The illusion that money makes the man is what is driving them. The devil tried to use the same trap on Jesus, showing him kingdoms, and their splendor. He could have them, He would be king over these kingdoms and be the ultimate 'Big Man'. Jesus though would not be sucked into the trap because He knew who He was and His call on the earth. His call was to worship God and serve him only with His time, talent and abilities. Our call is the same, to worship and serve God only, but if we fall into the temptation that the world system presents, we end up worshiping and serving it. We become slaves to the world system even if the world celebrates us.

## 5. The debt trap

Debt is one of the most sinister traps of the world system. A lot of people living in both developed and developing countries are in debt. Household debt which combines both mortgage debt and consumer debt as a percentage of disposable income stood at 205% of GDP in Australia, 308% in Denmark, 207% in Ireland, 283% in Netherlands and 166% in Canada[9]. Within the financial services industry, banks and other credit card companies are quite aggressive in marketing the debt products. In many countries, banks have direct sales representatives or direct marketing to sell consumer loans and particularly credit cards. Consumer loans are easily provided to people, from the newly employed youth to the shoppers in retail stores. These loans are marketed as a solution for the lifestyle people want now. These companies take out advertising spaces in various media outlets with attractive images of beautiful, healthy couples, who look happy with their stylish homes and new cars in the background. They use the power of subliminal messaging to associate the credit card with those things. A lot of people do not think there is anything wrong with credit cards or consumer loans; it affords them the lifestyle they want. But if you have to borrow to afford your lifestyle, isn't that a trap? It's just a matter of time before the house of card crumbles. Credit cards companies indicate that having debt levels of up to 20% of your annual income is fine. Do not fall for that trap. To a credit card company, your loan is an asset. It makes them money that is why they encourage you to pay the minimum possible. If you had $5,000 in credit card debt, it would take you over 40 years at interest rates of over 20% per year to repay it if you only paid the minimum amount! We discuss how to get out of the debt trap in subsequent chapters.

As you keep adding material possessions mistaking them for assets, you keep the cycle of expenses going. Even for those of you not in credit card debt, the push for a certain lifestyle through adverts and peer pressure will make you spend more than you need to just live this lifestyle. In the United States, owning your own home is the ultimate American dream. In the preceding years before the 2008 financial crisis, mortgage companies began to lend money even to people who had poor credit scores. They had low incomes or unsteady jobs or histories of not paying loans. Some even had no jobs. The estate agents and mortgage houses aggressively sought home buyers at whatever cost. The people, excited by the prospect of owning their own homes bought the sales pitch from these ' professionals' and were ignorant of the terms of these easy loans. The desire to fulfill the American dream; to be home owners was too strong and it was used to their disadvantage. The economy was growing and the home prices were going up. The real estate market was booming. When the economy began to slow down and the interest on these loans went up, the poor and middle class who had taken these loans were not able to service them. The default rates went up, leading to foreclosures. Families that put in their savings every month to paying their mortgages lost their savings and their homes. They couldn't even sell their houses to recover some money because everybody else was selling and the real estate market had crashed. This is what led to the financial crisis, debt. Once you are in debt getting out of it is an uphill task. Through payment of interest, you lose even the money you would have saved. Getting in is easy, getting out is the job.

# CHARACTERISTICS OF THE WORLD SYSTEM

The world system has certain traits, markers it can be identified by. Here are the characteristics of the world system:

- The world system has government or corporate entities with oppressive positions of rulership towards its citizens. People are at the mercy of the government. The people sell their liberties for a salary. Any system that causes you to look up to it for employment makes you to be at its mercy and is exploitative.

- A world system is a system of bondage that controls you through consumer debt, social security and health care systems.

- The world system is a system of exploitation, bondage and dominion of human beings even though one is selling their liberties freely. Any job or occupation that ties you down and deprives you of your will and freedom is part of this system. There is no fruit for your labor. Examine your life. Where is the past 5, 10, 20 years of your life tangibly? If you cannot account for that time you have been part of the world system.

Through money and its desires, the world system enslaves people. It's your desire to make money that makes you sell yourself to the world system. To whom ever you yield yourself as a servant to obey, you are his servant[10]. You are either a master of money or a slave to money. If you go to your job primarily because of the salary, you are a slave to money. To be a master of money you must be the one in charge of money. You must be able to direct money such that it does not determine where you can or cannot go, what you can or cannot eat, where to live and what to do with your life. Your life must be directed by God not money. Make sure you have so much money that you don't have to work for money. Make money work for you. Only less than 3% of the world has so much money they don't have to work. You, the reader are likely in the second category and must therefore make money work for you. If you are careful to put into practice the principles in this book, then you will eventually be free from having to work for money.

The world system does not teach you the laws of money. It teaches you to work hard and to spend money. The system is set up for you to be more and more engrossed in the need to make money. It pushes you to feel the need to look for money. For legitimate desires such as catering for the family, people sell themselves to the world system. The world is fast paced. People are becoming busier and busier with their occupations. They do not have time to think deep enough, to analyze their lives and what their actions entail. What is the result of their busyness? Without financial freedom, adding more responsibilities only entrenches you deeper into the bondage of the world system.

# IS THERE A WAY OUT?

There is an alternative to this world system as shown in scriptures. Jesus teaches us to pray that the Kingdom of God would come to the earth.

**"Thy kingdom come. Thy will be done on earth, as it is in heaven".**
*(Matthew 6:10)*

The Kingdom of God is the government of God. The government of God was meant to rule the world. It is when the righteous rule that the oppression of the world system would end.

**"When the righteous are in authority, the people rejoice: but when the wicked bear rule, the people mourn".**
*(Proverbs 29:2)*

We are to bring back the rule of God on the earth so that the world is set free from the god of this world. The kingdoms of this world are to become the kingdoms of our Lord and of His Christ[11].

Bringing back the rule of God is the greatness we are created for. Your greatness is in your uniqueness, your calling. Christians should only work with one purpose, to bring the kingdom of God into the sphere where He has called them. You are to strategize how to use your gifts and talents to bring God's government and ruler-ship and His right way (righteousness) into place. The original purpose of work was to bring God's Kingdom to bear in our workplace. God gave Adam a mandate, in the beginning to produce results, multiply and have dominion on the earth on God's behalf. We as sons of Adam inherited that mandate.

## WORK BUT DON'T GET TRAPPED

Work should be a service to God. If you have to work under someone, within a corporation, make sure you don't get trapped by the world system. Like Daniel in Babylon. He worked under an evil king, but right from the beginning he and his friends ensured they did not partake of the diet of Babylon. He did not bow to their gods; you must not bow to the gods of this world. My friends Raj and Thomas are trapped in their jobs and their plush lifestyles. They cannot fully pursue the mandate of God for their lives unless they set themselves free from the trap of the work system. If you are trapped make sure you pay yourself and build a secured financial future. Learn and understand the laws of money to ensure money works for you.

We were not created to hustle through life to make ends meet. The fruit of the world system is survival. All our potential dies and the only thing we have to show for our life is breathing. It is designed that way. To get a different result, we have to be deliberate to change our actions. Only a mad man does the same things expecting a different result.

If you like Raj are content still with your life now, read no further. Change comes to the one who is fed up!

To be free to serve God and fulfill your calling, you have to do everything to set yourself free from the captivity of money and the world system. We will discuss the strategies to set you free in subsequent chapters. It is important to remember that this book is a practical guide to set you free and break the ignorance the system uses to keep you in captivity. However the principles contained herein must be followed diligently to set you free.

We emphasize that before any change can happen, a person has to begin to see differently. Your life now, is as a result of the vision you have had consciously or unconsciously. Your ability to see is vital to this freedom. If you are in a financial crisis, what you have seen and how you see the world are ultimately responsible for where you are. The first step in the journey to freedom has to begin with your perspective. You have to change your paradigm, the prism from which you see and adopt the perspective of the Kingdom of God. Then change can begin.

## WAKE UP FROM YOUR SLUMBER

- If you keep receiving a salary but you cannot live without the salary you are trapped in the world system.

- The world system keeps you captive by enticing you using your own desires to spend the money you make. The American dream is not your ultimate dream. Comfort or luxury are good but should not be the culmination of your life.

- If you follow the desires of the world you will end up trapped in its system. Companies are after a piece of your income, if you follow what they tell you through advertising or peer pressure you will fall into their plan.

- You have no hope of getting out of the trap of the world system and building a secured financial future, if you do not pay yourself.

- You must be discontent with your life as it is now. You were not created to live for a house or a car or an affluent lifestyle no matter how comfortable. We all have a call from God for which we are to live. You have to seek the assignment of God for your life here on the earth.

- The assignment promotes God's agenda and expands the influence of God's government on the earth. In so doing the prayer in Mathew 6:10 is answered, as it is in heaven so it is on the earth.

- Through your assignment on the earth, you were meant to have dominion. As you become fruitful by producing goods and services, from your abilities and as you multiply your products, you multiply money, therefore you can have dominion in your area of calling.

That's the principle that big corporations have used to gain market shares. Companies such as Coca cola and Apple produced their drinks and phones and became excellent at production, to meet the demand in the market. As demand for these goods went up, they made more and more money and eventually became dominant players in their markets. Coca-Cola started in a small town with just a recipe, in a drug store in 1886. Founded by a bookkeeper, Frank Robinson and the man who created the recipe, pharmacist John Pemberton. Over 100 years, they got better and better at producing their cola drink and marketing the drink, they multiplied, become bigger and bigger. Coca cola is currently one of the largest beverage producers in the world.

# SELF ASSESSMENT TEST

Answer the following questions to do an inventory of your life:

1. What makes you get up in the morning?
2. Are you doing the job you are passionate about?
3. Do you know your purpose and are you living it?
4. What are you spending money on?
5. How many of the things you buy are things you need? How many of them are things you don't need but desired?
6. Do you have items purchased to boost your ego? What informs your desire? Get to the real reason you bought the car, or house or that gadget.
7. Where are the last 5, 10, 20 years of your life? Can you provide tangible evidence of what you have done with those years? This should not include marrying or having children because your ultimate reason for being on earth is God and His assignment not anything else.

If you have read through this first chapter and identified some of the bondage you are trapped in, you may experience the following. Sadness at having lost so many years of your life, hopelessness at being trapped by the expenses and responsibilities you bear and anger at not being able to do what you love. Take time to feel these emotions, and to let these emotions burn in you until you must seek a way out. If you are a prisoner, you have to turn these emotions into a strong desire to be free because if you are not free, you will live a life of sadness and regret. You must examine your life now and determine that is NOT the life you wish to continue to live.

# GOLDEN NUGGETS

- A world system is defined as a whole plan or scheme consisting of many parts connected in such a manner as to create a chain of mutual dependencies

- The world system is a trap that enslaves, people end up spending their lives living for food, shelter and clothing.

- Until you begin to see life differently, worldly desires will keep running you.

- For a man to escape the trap of the world system, he has to change his perspective on life.

- The pursuit of wealth is not what our time here on earth is for.

- Most people are not thinking about their purpose and even if they were, they cannot pursue purpose because their responsibilities and expenses cannot allow them

- Our call is to worship and serve God only but if we fall into the temptation that the world system presents, we end up worshiping and serving it. We become slaves to the world system even if the world celebrates us.

- We were not created to hustle through life to make ends meet.

# CHAPTER 2

# IMPORTANCE OF PAYING YOURSELF

## YOUR FUTURE DEPENDS ON THE CHOICES YOU MAKE TODAY

As we have defined the world system, we have determined that most people are not living their lives for God. In fact if you have analyzed your life based on the questions at the end of Chapter 1, you will realize that you too may not be living for God and the purpose for which He placed you here on the earth. Yes, you love God but because bills control you, you are not able to love your God with all your heart, all your soul and with your entire mind and with all your strength[12]. If you cannot do as Jesus did; He did everything God told him to do[13] , you are trapped. If God told you to move from your current job to a lower paying job in your area of passion, would you be able to? Do you have the freedom and boldness to say no to practices within your job that do not agree with the leading of God, without fear of losing your job? Are you able to give your family, your children the quality time they require to be godly offspring?[14] If your answer is no to any of these questions, then you need to find a way out. Set yourself free from the thing that stops you. Build a secured financial future.

This is why it is important to pay yourself. Let me first define what 'pay yourself' means and correct some of the

41

wrong perceptions of what people think it means. To pay yourself means to set aside money that you earn however frequently; daily or monthly. Paying yourself does not refer to the amount of money you have left after your various expenditures. You set aside money for paying yourself only after giving your tithes and offerings but before deducting your expenses. This money is your savings which will be used to make investments. As we have seen, the world is built to entrap you into receiving a salary or income but never being free from it. To never being financially free. To escape this trap, you need to outsmart this system by learning to deliberately set aside an amount of money every month towards meeting your goal of financial independence.

# MYTHS ABOUT PAYING YOURSELF

There is a popular saying in the world when referring to salary. We say we earn an income. This leads people to believe that because they earn money, they are paying themselves.

### 1. HAVING A SALARY OR HAVING AN INCOME IS NOT EQUAL TO PAYING YOURSELF.

The first thing that happens when your income is allocated to you is that the government pays itself, through taxes. Then there are other deductions made depending on your country. They may include life insurance, car insurance and medical insurance and pension contributions. Again because you may be contributing towards your pension, you would conclude that you are paying yourself. Most times the money set aside towards your pension is not adequate to cater for your needs when you retire. If you only focus on your pension contribution, it is also likely to entrap you into staying in your job and not pursuing anything else. You must resist the urge to be comfortable.

## 2. TO PAY YOURSELF DOES NOT MEAN TO 'REWARD' YOURSELF BY BUYING YOURSELF LIABILITIES THAT STROKE YOUR EGO.

Remember my friend Raj? This summer, Raj and his family went on a weeklong vacation to the Caribbean. Raj believes that because he works so many hours a week and does not get to see his family as much as he would want to, a vacation is the perfect way to reward himself for all that hard work and sacrifice. Plus he gets to spend time with his family. Paying yourself means you must acquire assets and reduce your liabilities. Assets are things that bring money into your pockets. If Raj had saved the vacation money and took his family on a more modest holiday, he would have been able to set aside over $10,000 to buy assets. Liabilities are those things that take money from you. When you put aside money for your future you are paying yourself and building a secured financial future. When you set aside money for your children's future; for school fees and such, you are paying yourself. When you set aside money towards your calling, you are paying yourself and building a secured financial future.

### 3. PAYING YOURSELF IS NOT LIMITED ONLY TO THOSE WHO ARE EMPLOYED.

Small and medium enterprises make up the larger part of economic growth across Africa and other developing countries. Some people work on a freelance basis and therefore do not have a regular salary. To be able to pay yourself and build a secure financial future, you need to know what your necessary expenses are at any given month and save all amounts above your necessary expenses. On low seasons, what if your income is not enough to pay your basic expenses for a month? This is why it is important to build a passive income from your investments so that you are not relying on your salary or active income to live. It gives you freedom to focus on growing your business.

A lot of people have a good income and have no money left after paying their bills. In this case you are living from paycheck to paycheck. You have paid your landlord, your electricity company, the water company, schools, the shop where you buy your clothes, the salon where your hair is done and everybody else except yourself. Don't just work for others; make sure you are working for yourself and building your future.

Paying yourself involves setting aside at least 30% towards your future through savings and investment. If you are married or have children, a beginning target of at least 10% of your income is doable. Grow this target to 30% as soon as you can, depending on your responsibilities. However aim to save at least 50% of your income. If you are not married and do not have children, aim to start saving at least 30% of your income and target to grow to 70% of your income. This will help you reach you goals faster and help you break free from the trap of the world system earlier.

Becoming a millionaire is a numbers game. Every Christian can and should become one. This begins first with how much money you are able to pay yourself regularly to secure your financial future. Then how much is put in investments, earning a good return, at least 20% per year. We will look at how this can be achieved in the chapter on investments.

Please note here that the goal of savings is to invest not for savings sake. Once you have accumulated enough money in savings, you have to then make the decision to invest depending on your financial plan. You have to make sure your investments are making money. Jesus teaches in the parable of the sower that not all of the scattered seeds germinate. Some seeds fall on rocky ground and others on foot paths and do not germinate. Of those seeds that do germinate some are chocked by thorn bushes. Only a few bear fruits, but of the fruits they bring forth, it is enough to cover for the loss of some seeds. When making investments, you need to follow the same principle. Diversify your investments to ensure that the profit from your investments would be enough to cover for any loss you may incur on some investments. We will look at more of this in the chapter on investments.

Save money despite expenses. Someone may ask, I don't earn enough money to save, how can I set aside money when I have so many expenses? The reason you set aside money is to build your future. If you do not find money to save, you will be unable to break free from the cycle of living from income to income, salary to salary trying to make ends meet. If the sower had eaten his seeds, he would not have received 30, 60 and 100 times as much as he had planted. You have to be determined within yourself to find ways to save money. We will look at how to in the following chapter on savings.

# YOUR TICKET OUT OF POVERTY

There is a cost to being poor, unfortunately. For most countries around the world, the cost of living for poor people is higher than for the rich and the middle class. Loans are more expensive, with higher interest rates charged while goods bought in small quantities by the poor do not benefit from economies of scale. If you have ever visited a slum in the developing world or a low income neighborhood in the developed world, you will identify certain things that are very prevalent there. There are many dysfunctional homes and absentee fathers and the results are high levels of prostitution, violence, murder and crime. Poverty reduces human beings to subhuman creatures. It robs them of the dignity endowed on them by their creator. Paying yourself is your ticket out of poverty to a secured financial future.

If your earnings are meager, it is even more critical for you to set aside money. You can use this money to invest in yourself, to start a new business, to improve your skills and to know the laws of money. This is the only way you could increase your earning and break away from the cycle of poverty. If your income is less than the minimum wage in your country, you may first have to seek for ways to increase your income while maintaining or even reducing your current standard of living. You need to educate your mind first because the primary cause of poverty is ignorance.

A house maid in a certain *third world* nation found some outdated unused notes, equivalent to less than a dollar. Because they were no longer used as legal tender, she approached her employer, to see if the employer could give her the equivalent worth in the new currency. What she did not know was that these notes were now collectables worth hundreds of dollars. Because of ignorance, she exchanged these outdated notes for a few dollars. You probably have lost opportunities like this maid did before. Maybe you did not even notice that you were missing out on opportunities. If you do not educate yourself you will keep missing such opportunities. By reading books and listening to talks by people who have broken free, you can educate yourself and be able to spot opportunities when they come. Invest in books from public libraries or in the internet to educate yourself.

There are now opportunities to make money by providing freelance services through the internet. Take an inventory of your time and make efficient use of your time at work. Use your spare hours to take up a part time job, or freelance work that can increase your income. Once you have spent time educating your mind, you will be able to spot opportunities to make additional income. You could borrow stock from a wholesale and retail it to your colleagues at work during office breaks and keep the profits. Opportunity comes to the mind that is prepared.

## PAY YOURSELF WHEN YOU HAVE NO JOB

What if you have no job? If you have no job, you have a valuable commodity called time. As discussed earlier it is important to do an inventory of your life. Look at your abilities; have you developed your abilities enough to easily turn them into goods or services? Take time to develop these goods or services and sell them to create money. What skills can you use to your advantage? If you are very outgoing and social, you can easily sell a product or a service that you are passionate about. Some of the world's wealthiest people are sales people. Sales is a highly sought after skill as every non-profit organization in the world is seeking to sell its goods for profit. If you can refine this skill you can work and generate good commissions while still maintaining some of your time, freedom and autonomy. The extra time you have should be used to explore more into your calling, refine your gifts and build your business. Make sure you are setting aside money to pay yourself even as you look to transition to your area of calling. Secure your financial future even when you don't have a job. The purpose here is to set yourself free so that you can pursue your calling. Make sure money eventually works for you and you are not forced to work for money.

Four young men, in one of the developing countries in the world found themselves unable to find jobs and in poverty. As they looked around their neighborhood they noticed an interesting trend. Most of the people who had jobs left their homes very early in the morning, before 6am to beat the city's traffic jam. Because they left so early they did not have time to take breakfast and since they could not afford the high prices in the city, they did not eat all day. These young men decided to address this problem. They borrowed $50 from a youth co-operative in their country and bought cooking equipment and government licenses. They began to make simple snacks which they would sell for less than a dollar. They open their stall at 4am and prepare and pack the snacks. By 8am every morning they made at least 25$ each. Each month they would make at least $500 which is equivalent to a teacher's salary in a developing country. From these proceeds the young men were able to enroll in a college. The oldest of them now runs an IT consulting firm in the city while the rest of the young men are still in college. They continue to run their snack shop. They have been able to make various investments and because they do not have to rely on a job, they are free to set up their own businesses in their areas of passion.

One of the common complaints by employers particularly against millennials; young people below the age of 30, is the quality of the work they produce. Most people do the bare minimum. Out of hundreds, only one or two people are able to produce quality work. Make it your goal to develop yourself to the level that you can produce exceptional work, and differentiate yourself by your level of excellence.

Catherine, a daughter to one of our church members attended one of our churches with her mother. She had just finished high school and did not have any money to go to college. She picked up a book written by a church member with some of the life principles I taught and she studied it thoroughly. Before she turned 18, she took up a menial job at a car wash company. She made up her mind to apply what she had learnt and to do her very best. While working there, she did her jobs diligently and consistently. She did not complain or refuse any work and she made sure she did her work as fast as she could and with excellence. Eventually the company owners noticed her and promoted her to manage the other employees. She continued to be diligent at her work and she became so effective that she overtook the general manager at the company in terms of results. The bosses then decided to make her the managing director of the company at age 19. From her salary she saved money and she's been paying her college fees at the university where she has been studying the last couple of years. She paid herself and she is now building her future by pursuing a degree in Finance and Economics, her area of interest. Irrespective of your circumstances, whether you are employed or self-employed or jobless, you too can learn the principles to pay yourself and build your future.

Africa has some of the world's highest unemployment rates. In some countries, the unemployment rate is as high as 54% of the population[15]. Most of these people are largely young people below the age of 30 years. The education systems in these countries do not prepare these youth for entrepreneurship or to develop jobs for themselves, and so many believe they can only have an income once they are employed. They have seen generations of their parents and grandparents spend their years being employed by someone else for a salary. Because of this mindset they are unable to take advantage of opportunities around them and convert them to money. Social media provides a lot of opportunities for an entrepreneurial mind. There are online platforms suitable to advertise and sell your goods. Other platforms provide opportunities to offer services. Even if you felt you do not have a lot of talents, if you have a functioning brain you can provide a good or service by using your mind.

For example, you can cook certain foods and sell them via online marketing, generating a higher income than if you sold in your neighborhood. In fact, if you have some cooking or cleaning skills, you can set up a Facebook page or a YouTube channel where you can give advice on how to cook or clean well. YouTube allows you to make money from you videos depending on how many viewers you get. Opportunities other than the internet are available particularly in the developing world. Opportunity sometimes comes wrapped up in problems. What are the problems in your area, and do you have the solutions? Sell these solutions to create money. Like the four young men in our earlier example, identify a solution to the problems in your area and make money from selling the solutions, no matter how small. There are many emerging opportunities to make money; you need to engage your brain in much thought to dig up these opportunities. Do not allow yourself to fall into excuses or pity parties; that will be a deep ditch to get out of.

Use prayer; Communion with God to encourage yourself, to discover yourself and to get new ideas on how to solve the problems in your life. Remember that God is your strength and your exceeding great reward[16]. If you have God, you have all the answers. Seek His will on the issues you are currently dealing with and once you get a leading from him on how to move forward, take action. Don't procrastinate. Do not let prayers be your excuse for not taking actions at the right time. When you experience failure, go back to God and His word for encouragement. When you are worried, raise your worries up to God, so that you can have peace. Lack of peace, discouragement and depression are some of the things that might drive you to spend money to relieve your discomfort. Binge eating and shopping addiction are some of the things driven by stresses of life. When your mind is at peace, you are able to see solutions and opportunities more easily. Invest in time with God, you have the mind of Christ and can tap into it for answers to any problem. Knowing who you are will deliver you from peer pressure and the cultural pressure that leads us to waste money. It also shields you from loving money and becoming a slave to money.

During the stressful time at work, Thomas, my friend discovered the gospel of the kingdom and began to pray about his problem at work. At first he would only pray concerning the investigations at his job and that he would retain his job. With time he realized his job had become a trap to him, he was terrified of losing it. He knew he had to do something about it. He had to confront the fear of losing his job and begin to insure himself against the dependence on his salary. Through prayer, his eyes were opened to the trap he was in. Even though he was making a good salary, he could not afford to lose his job. He has started on the journey to change his situation.

## MAKING MONEY ISN'T PAYING YOURSELF

We have seen over time however, that making a lot of money does not make you financially independent and does not build a secured financial future. American NBA[17] basketball players are some of the highest paid athletes in the world and yet 60% of the players are broke within the first 5 years of retirement[18]. 78% of former National Football League, NFL players are in financial crisis or bankrupt within the first 2 years of retirement. The reason is attributed to ignorance about money and poor financial habits and decisions concerning their earnings. Most of those athletes spend money extravagantly and are uninterested in learning about savings and investments.

If you do not learn to pay yourself, you have no hope of becoming financially independent and having secured financial future, no matter how much you make. You cannot come out of financial crisis or debt. You can only be likened to the poor farmer who eats all his seeds from his harvest. He does not set aside seeds for the next planting season. He will have nothing to plant in that season and his future is doomed. Even if he had reduced his eating to the bare minimum, unlike the sower he has no hope for 30, 60 or 100 times more in harvest. Paying yourself ensures you do not eat tomorrow's food today. When you don't pay yourself you are trapped working for others.

It is through the principle of saving and then investment that you can be set free from reliance on salary and build a secured financial future. Once you don't need a salary to earn money, you can then be free to work within your calling. The reason so many people are not able to follow their purpose is because they need a salary and what they are passionate about may not make them money at the beginning. Let's say you are an accountant by training but your call is as a musician. You need time to develop your gift as a musician, to learn to package yourself and your music, market it and be accepted in the market place. In the process of training and development you may not be able to make much from your gift. If you had investments working for you, generating money for you, you could be able to quit your job, enroll in a music school or join a band to increase your skills and experience in music.

It is because of the future that you see once you understand your calling, that you sacrifice today. You sacrifice today's comfort by cutting down your expenditure, scaling down your lifestyle, so that you can build the vision God has put in your heart. When I was starting out my ministry in Kyiv, Ukraine, I quit a well paying job because I realized I could not handle both the ministry and my career in journalism. I had to move out of my two bedroom apartment, gave up my car and moved into a students' hostel so that I could focus on building the ministry. I was able to live on the money I had paid myself while I had an income. I have succeeded in building the largest evangelical Christian church network across Europe. Determine to apply the principles I show you here, you too will be free to pursue your calling.

## PAY YOURSELF DESPITE DEBT

How do you save despite being in debt? You need to get out of debt while you save. To get out of debt you need to stop digging. Stop getting into more debt. The law of compounding works for you when you are investing but works against you when you are in debt. The higher the interest charged the more you will pay when paying off your original debt. This is what you can do:

1. **Look at your expenses, and make a plan on how to drastically scale down on your lifestyle.**

Can you move to a cheaper house and save cash within a month? Do you have things you could sell off; cars, electronics, clothes and such? Set time a frame within which you wish to do so and stick to it.

2. **Do not buy any new things unless absolutely necessary.** Take time to plan to buy necessary needs and stick to the plan. Do not eat out. Carry packed lunch or eat at home. Look to discount items or sales when buying necessary things like food and household items.

3. **Use the money saved to begin to pay off your debt.** However, do not use all your money to pay your debt, use up to 20% of your income to pay off your debt. Calculate the time it will take to pay off all your debt after you have scaled down on your lifestyle and stick to it. We will look at the steps to get out of debt later on in the book.

4. **Make it a principle not to lend money.** You are not a bank or a lending institution. The problem with lending when you are not licensed to lend is that you have no way to compel people to pay you back. You are completely under the mercy of your debtor, whether they pay you or not is solely their decision. Only lend money that you do not expect to receive back.

# PAY GOD FIRST

It is important to remember however that we do not pay ourselves first. We 'pay' God first. To Christians, it is actually honoring God with their fruitfulness, which is their income. Why is this important and why do we do it first? Let's look at some of the stories from the Bible of people who honored God first through giving and how they were able to please God as a result. We start with the story of Cain and Abel. In Genesis 4, Abel offers to God the firstborn of his flock, but Cain offers the fruit of the ground, not necessarily the first fruit. The first fruit was the form of tithe then, the first part of your income. God rejects Cain's offering because it wasn't the first fruit and accepts Abel's because it was the first. Abel's sacrifice pleased God and he was able to live a life of significance. This giving was done first to honor God and his offering was accepted because he did it well, verse 7 and Cain's was rejected because he didn't do it as it should have been done. Cain, even though he built cities, was a wanderer and did not fulfill the purpose of God for him. In the same way, you may seem busy making achievements but if you are not pursuing your calling your life is of no relevance to God and His Kingdom.

From the story of the second generation of inhabitants on the earth, we see that they had already built in themselves a culture of honoring God first with their giving. This was likely learnt from their parents, Adam and Eve. The practice of giving God first from your income is likened to a manufacturer who puts a foolproof mechanism in his gadget to prevent it from malfunctioning. Giving to God first builds in you a safeguard, to prevent you from worshiping money.

In another example, we see even before Moses was given the law, the custom of giving a tenth of their income was an ancient practice to worship the object of the giving. The people of God gave a tenth of their income to God first to honor him and acknowledge their reliance on Him. Abraham gave a tenth of his spoils to Melchizedek, King of Salem and priest of God in worship. His descendant Jacob in Bethel makes a promise to God to give Him a tenth of everything God gives him as worship[19]. Abraham went on to fulfill his call as a father of nations. He was a man that God trusted that he would order his family after God. Jacob became Israel upon whom the nation was founded. These men were free to pursue the call of God for their lives.

Today many people have abused the practice of first fruit by giving it to the pastor. First fruits should be given to your parents and people who helped you to become who you are. If your parents are well off you can give it to the poor, destitute and needy people. You should not give your first fruits to pastors. Your first fruits should be used in the service of people like Jesus commanded.

**Now behold, I have brought the first of the produce of the ground which You, O LORD have given me.' And you shall set it down before the LORD your God, and worship before the LORD your God; and you and the Levite and the alien who is among you shall rejoice in all the good which the LORD your God has given you and your household.**

**"When you have finished [a]paying all the tithe of your increase in the third year, the year of tithing, then you shall give it to the Levite, to the stranger, to the orphan and to the widow, that they may eat in your [c]towns and be satisfied.**

*(Deuteronomy 26:10-12)*

In the culture of the day as evidenced throughout the scripture, one of the practices of the Israelites was to kill a fattened calf or lamb in honor of a visitor. They were taking a portion of their wealth and giving it away as a way to honor the visitor. Such forms of giving are still practiced today and are prevalent among various tribes in Africa and the Middle East. Giving God or His cause therefore is a way we honor God. In honoring God first we also experience one of the key blessings from God; He preserves us from worshipping mammon. The Bible teaches us that we can never serve two masters. It is either we are serving God or we are serving mammon[20]. When we offer sacrifices in forms of tithes and offerings with pure hearts to God, we cannot then worship money because we have demonstrated by giving it away that we value more the one to whom we have given. This is the first principle in mastering money. You must worship God, not money. Whoever determines your actions is who or what you worship.

The amount you should give as tithe is 10% of your income and offerings should be at least 5% of your income but should be guided by the leading of God. There are a lot of teachings concerning giving in many churches across the world that are manipulative and engineered to make you give these pastors as much of your money as possible. Do not fall for these teachings. Only give what God is directing you to give. Many people have lost their homes, given their schools fees in the name of 'sowing seed' to receive blessing or for financial breakthrough only to end up impoverished. The 'seed sowing' is not sowing into your future; it is only paying the churches and the pastors.

# BABY STEPS TO BEGIN WITH

1. Invest time to know God and His word. The more you know God, the more you know who you are and can withstand the pressure to worship money. The world system is set up to make you a slave to money and to make you live according to the dictates of money.

2. Take responsibility for the current state of your life. Admit you were wrong and stop making excuses. Excuses are the trademark of a failure. When you make excuses you abdicate from the ability to change your situation.

3. To overcome financial crisis, you must first overcome the poverty of the mind. Invest time and money to educate yourself on the laws of money, on discovering your calling and developing your gifts and abilities into usable skills.

4. If your expenses exceed your income, you are never going to be financially free. Learn how to manage money so that it doesn't make you its servant. Master yourself and don't spend money emotionally. The way you spend money may be what is causing your financial crisis.

5. Do not allow material things to define who you are. Your worth is not determined by the abundance of your possessions. Know who you are. Stop spending money on what you don't have to impress people who don't care. Live below your means until you have money working for you.

6. Find new ways to be frugal. Not mean, frugal.

There is a difference. Frugality is cutting out spending on what you don't need, meanness is eliminating spending on things you need like insurance, healthcare and healthy food. Never spend on what you can do without. Ask yourself, if I don't spend on this will it cost me? Will I die? If not don't spend it. Draw a list of things or people who are taking money from you and cross them out one by one until you only have the necessary ones.

7. Distribute your income in order of importance in percentages, starting with God then yourself. Give 10% of your income to God in tithes and 5% in offerings. Create a culture of saving at least 30% of your income. If you are overburdened by debt, begin at 10% and grow into 30% of your income.

8. Create money. Find new ways to increase your income. Engage your mind and engage God for new money making ideas. Manage your time well to have more time for the new money making opportunities.

9. The purpose of saving is not just saving but to invest. Begin to invest the money saved as soon as possible.

To recap, we have seen that your financial fulfillment is not dependent on how much you make but how successful you are in managing the resources you have. We have busted the myths that surround the concept of paying yourself. Paying yourself is setting aside money to invest towards your future. Anything else is just expenses. Do not delude yourself into thinking that you are paying yourself because you earn a salary or you buy 'stuffs' for yourself. Only savings and investments qualify as paying yourself. You note that I did not indicate you pay yourself first. You pay God first to honor and worship him and to preserve yourself from worshipping money.

In the next chapter we would look at the technicalities of paying yourself. How do you save money? If you are like most people you have tried to save money, probably more than once and failed. How do you ensure you succeed in saving money? I will now show you tricks to use to guarantee success in savings.

# GOLDEN NUGGETS

- To escape the trap of the system, you need to outsmart this it by learning to deliberately set aside an amount of money every month towards meeting your goal of financial independence.

- You must resist the urge to be comfortable.

- When you put aside money for your future, you are paying yourself and building a secured financial future.

- Don't just work for others; make sure you are working for yourself and building your future.

- Poverty reduces human beings to subhuman creatures. It robs them of the dignity endowed on them by their creator.

- If your earnings are meager, it is even more critical for you to set aside money.

- The primary cause of poverty is ignorance of the mind.

- There are many emerging opportunities to make money; you need to engage your brain in much thought to dig up these opportunities.

- Don't procrastinate. let praying not be your excuse for lack of action.

- It is through the principle of saving and then investment that you can be set free from reliance on salary and build a secured financial future

- It is because of the future that you see once you understand your calling, that you sacrifice today.

- Today many people have abused the practice of first fruit by giving it to the pastor.

- Give only what God is directing you to give.

# CHAPTER 3

# THE DISCIPLINE OF SAVING

*"I would venture to say lack of personal self-discipline is the number one delineating factor between the rich, the poor and middle class"*
*Robert Kiyosaki, Author of Rich Dad, Poor Dad.*

Robert Kiyosaki is a respected author. In his best-selling book Rich Dad, Poor Dad he makes a comparison between his two mentors and how their life's philosophy influenced whether they succeeded at building wealth or not. In his experiences he summarizes personal self-discipline as a key reason why some people are rich and others are poor. If you lack self-discipline, you will end up poor.

Now that you understand the importance of paying yourself, where do we begin? Saving is your first step to financial freedom.

The story is told of a worker in the United States, Elinor Sauerwein[21], who at the time of her death had amassed almost 2 million US dollars. She had worked as a teacher, a cook and for a machines company. None of the jobs were high income jobs; in fact some were quite menial. She started saving this money with one goal, to give to the Salvation Army's work. Upon her death, her estate gave $1,731,533 in December 2011 to a California branch of the Salvation Army. How did she manage this while her jobs were and are still among the lowest income paying jobs in the United States? Elinor was born in the early 1900's and by the time she was finishing college the great depression had wrecked a havoc on the job market. She was taught as she grew up never to waste anything and practiced frugality almost to an extreme. She would dry her laundry on a clothesline in her backyard, saving on both a dryer and electricity. She would do her own household repairs and maintenance. She would not go to restaurants or the movies or pay for cable TV because *'every dollar I save is another dollar that could go to the Salvation Army.'* When she got married both she and her husband continued the practice of frugality. Harold Sauerwein, her husband and a contractor, built their home with his own two hands. Elinor grew her own fruits and vegetables in her backyard garden and would pick them herself even at old age. She took a vacation only once in her life and considered it a spending spree. The people around her thought she was poor because she lived like she was poor. Elinor and Harold invested their savings in various business opportunities and Elinor continued in this practice even after her husband's death. Elinor's story should inspire you to look for foxes in your expenses that are eating your money and eliminate them. If she could save money, you too can save money through some of the principles of being frugal. Your ability to save should be driven by your goal. Like Elinor, you should be able to say, every coin saved is another coin to pay myself and set me free to advance God's Kingdom. We will look at setting financial goals to fuel your savings in the coming paragraphs.

# HOW TO START SAVING

Bills and expenses are one of the key tools used by Satan to control people. Bills and expenses want to be your master. The temptation is to make bills the focus of your life, what you are living for. The first thing you do when you get your salary is to pay your bills. If you are paying 50 to 70% of your income towards meeting your bills, you are a slave to those bills. If you say you cannot save because you have many bills you are saying you don't care about your future. You have resigned yourself to a life where bills control you, to being a slave forever. If you want your freedom, you have to do whatever it takes to save money. How do you go about doing this?

1. Make an inventory of everything you have to pay for right now. Be as detailed as possible. List all your general expenses. Here is an example:

Expenses this Month

| ITEM | EXPENSES | MONTHLY TOTAL |
|---|---|---|
| GIVING | | |
| | Tithes and Offerings | |
| | Family giving | |
| SHELTER & COMMUNICATION | | |
| | Rent | |
| | House repairs | |
| | Life insurance | |
| | Utilities (like electricity and gas) | |
| | Internet, cable TV, and phones | |

| | | |
|---|---|---|
| | Other housing expenses (like property taxes) | |
| | Prepaid cards and phone cards | |
| **FOOD** | | |
| | Groceries and house-hold shopping | |
| | Eating out | |
| **Transport** | | |
| | Public transportation | |
| | Taxis | |
| | Fuel | |
| | Parking and toll fees | |
| | Car maintenance | |
| | Car insurance | |
| | Car loan repayments | |
| | Train or air ticket costs | |
| **HEALTH** | | |
| | Medicine | |
| | Health insurance | |
| | Other health expenses | |
| | Gym | |
| **FAMILY & SOCIAL NEEDS** | | |
| | Child care | |
| | Servants; House maid, gardener | |
| | Money given to family friends | |
| | School Fees | |
| **PERSONAL DEVELOPMENT** | | |
| | Educational Materials | |
| | Laptops | |

| CLOTHING | | |
|---|---|---|
| | Clothing and shoes | |
| | Dry Cleaning | |
| | Accessories plus Jewelry | |
| ENTERTAINMENT | | |
| | Entertainment (like movies and concerts) | |
| | Holidays and travel | |
| | Gifts | |
| | Parties | |
| | Hobbies | |
| | Pets | |
| | Club membership | |
| PERSONAL CARE | | |
| | Manicure, pedicure, facials | |
| | Hair | |
| | Shaving | |
| | Massage & spa | |
| | Cosmetics | |
| BANK FEES AND LOANS | | |
| | Cheques, transfers fees | |
| | Bank fees | |
| | Loan processing fees & penalties | |
| | School fees | |
| | Student loans | |
| | Credit cards payments | |
| | Other Debt | |
| | **Total monthly expenses** | $ |

2. Out of these expenses, identify your compulsory expenses. When you write down your expenses as in the above example, you discover things that you are spending money on that you do not need. I am sure also a lot of you may not have exact figures on where or what you are spending your money on. When doing the first step for now you can estimate what your expenses are. Over the next month however track your daily expenses. If you have a smartphone you can use one of the many expense tracking applications to detail daily your expenses. If you use a computer, you can download a Microsoft Excel spreadsheet that can also help you to do the same. If you are married, make sure you begin the process together with your spouse so that you are on the same page about your finances and the changes to be made.

3. Cancel out all the expenses in the paper that can be eliminated. From the above example, expenses such as eating out, personal care such as pedicures and facials, clothing and shoes can be eliminated. Write expenses that can be deferred. Holidays and travel can be deferred to a later time or you could travel to nearby places that cost very little just to keep your children entertained. A trip to the zoo, a picnic and the like. By doing this exercise you are restoring your authority over your income.

4. Indicate your priority expenses starting with God as number one and your purpose and calling as second. Put compulsory expenses as priorities and transfer your money to make your payments.

Don't rush to pay your expenses, stretch out your payments. Defer expenses that can be paid later.

**Priority Expenses**

| Expenses | Monthly Total |
|---|---|
| Tithes and Offerings | |
| PAY YOURSELF | |
| Housing; Rent/ Mortgage | |
| Life Insurance | |
| Utilities ( electricity and gas) | |
| Property taxes and house maintenance | |
| Groceries and household supplies | |
| Public transportation and taxis | |
| Medicine | |
| Health insurance | |
| Other health expenses (like eyeglasses) | |
| Child care | |
| Bank fees | |
| School Fees | |
| Student Loans | |
| Other Debts | |
| Total monthly expenses | |

5. Begin negotiating with people or institutions you owe money and rearrange terms of payment. Don't get into any new debt obligations.

6. List all possible future expenses. Try to anticipate as many expenses as you think might arise. These may include phone expenses, internet expenses,

ceremonies like birthdays and weddings and eating out with friends. Begin to do everything possible to avoid such additional expenses. If unexpected events like funerals occur, keep your expenditure as low as possible. The later chapters will also show you how to use some insurance products to secure your money.

7. Have a plan as to how to handle dependants. This is particularly for those with dependants in the extended family. Siblings and other relatives might constantly need your help. Work out a plan on how to assist in terms of a monthly percentage or invest on their behalf instead. If your parents are dependent on you, work out how to provide for them in the budget.

8. Learn to do without. Do you really need your mobile phone all the time? Can you cut out call costs and use free services such as Skype and other free tools to communicate? Other expenses you should consider cutting include use of first class transport for air and train travels. Unless your employer is paying for your travel or you have to travel for work purposes. Cut out all unnecessary travels also. That includes trips you make with your car, Sunday afternoon drives and the like.

9. Plan how to automatically pay your bills. Have bank instructions to pay your tithe, to transfer your savings into a separate account, settle rent and so on.

10. Begin to find ways to increase your assets and

reduce your liabilities. Your financial freedom depends on how much you are able to reduce expenses. The key to savings is not in how much you earn but in how little you spend. Look critically at what you are spending on. From your current expenses, find a way to increase your pay-yourself money to 15%. Do this each month until you can raise it to 30%. Cut insignificant little expenses. People spend small amounts of money without even being conscious of it. Snacks such as chocolates, sweets, cakes and coffees and soft drinks may take up to as much as 5$ a day. If you can save that money, it adds up to 150$ a month and 1,800$ a year. Stop all spending on luxury goods; wrist watches, jewelry are all things you can live without. Replace your restaurant lunch expenses with the cheaper option of home cooked meals. If you save all your lunch money, you may be saving 10$ a day and 200 to 300$ a month which adds up to $2,400 to $3,600 a year. Do the same with eating out expenses for the family. Instead of going out twice a week to a restaurant for a family treat, get cooking videos and learn to cook different meals as a family. You still get to spend time together and enjoy new kinds of foods for less. If you invested the money saved so far, up to 5,400$ and got a 20% interest per year, that translates to $13,436 in five years. That's just from small expenses. Look at the table below. If you saved $2,000 only and put it to work for you at 30% per year, you would have $27,572 in ten years and $102,372 in fifteen years without making any additional contributions. This is the power of compound interest. You have to make it work for you, even with the smallest savings. Do not just save money though. If you had kept the $2,000 in your bank account, in 10 years it would still be $2,000!

| Year | Return on Investment | | |
|---|---|---|---|
| | 10% p.a | 20% p.a | 30% p.a |
| Start | 2,000 | 2,000 | 2,000 |
| 1 | 2,200 | 2,400 | 2,600 |
| 2 | 2,420 | 2,880 | 3,380 |
| 3 | 2,662 | 3,456 | 4,394 |
| 4 | 2,928 | 4,147 | 5,712 |
| 5 | 3,221 | 4,977 | 7,426 |
| 6 | 3,543 | 5,972 | 9,654 |
| 7 | 3,897 | 7,166 | 12,550 |
| 8 | 4,287 | 8,600 | 16,315 |
| 9 | 4,716 | 10,320 | 21,209 |
| 10 | 5,187 | 12,383 | 27,572 |
| 11 | 5,706 | 14,860 | 35,843 |
| 12 | 6,277 | 17,832 | 46,596 |
| 13 | 6,905 | 21,399 | 60,575 |
| 14 | 7,595 | 25,678 | 78,748 |
| 15 | 8,354 | 30,814 | 102,372 |

It is time and consistency that makes money to grow. Suppose you were to save just 2,000 per year at the rate of return of 30% per year? You will have actually saved only 30,000$ but your money would have grown to over $ 500,000 in 15 years.

| Year | Return on Investment | | |
|---|---|---|---|
| | 10% p.a | 20% p.a | 30% p.a |
| Total saved | 30,000 | 30,000 | 30,000 |
| 1 | 2,200 | 2,400 | 2,600 |
| 2 | 4,620 | 5,280 | 5,980 |
| 3 | 7,282 | 8,736 | 10,374 |
| 4 | 10,210 | 12,883 | 16,086 |
| 5 | 13,431 | 17,860 | 28,686 |
| 6 | 16,974 | 23,832 | 39,892 |
| 7 | 20,872 | 30,998 | 54,459 |
| 8 | 25,159 | 39,598 | 73,397 |
| 9 | 29,875 | 68,949 | 98,016 |
| 10 | 35,062 | 85,139 | 130,021 |
| 11 | 40,769 | 104,567 | 171,628 |
| 12 | 47,045 | 127,880 | 225,716 |
| 13 | 53,950 | 155,856 | 296,031 |
| 14 | 61,545 | 189,427 | 387,440 |
| 15 | 69,899 | 229,713 | 506,272 |

Suppose you increase your savings to $1,000 per month that is 12,000 per year for 15 years?

| Year | Total saved | Return on Investment | | |
|---|---|---|---|---|
| | | 10% p.a | 20% p.a | 30% p.a |
| Annual savings | 12,000 | 12,000 | 12,000 | 12,000 |
| 1 | 12,000 | 13,200 | 14,400 | 15,600 |
| 2 | 24,000 | 27,720 | 31,680 | 35,880 |
| 3 | 36000 | 43,692 | 52,416 | 62,244 |
| 4 | 48,000 | 61,261 | 77,299 | 96,517 |

| 5 | 60,000 | 80,587 | 107,159 | 141,072 |
|---|---|---|---|---|
| 6 | 72,000 | 101,846 | 142,991 | 198,994 |
| 7 | 84000 | 125,231 | 185,989 | 274,292 |
| 8 | 96,000 | 150,954 | 237,587 | 372,180 |
| 9 | 108,000 | 179,249 | 413,695 | 499,434 |
| 10 | 120,000 | 210,374 | 510,834 | 664,864 |
| 11 | 132000 | 244,611 | 627,401 | 879,923 |
| 12 | 144,000 | 282,273 | 767,281 | 1,159,500 |
| 13 | 156,000 | 323,700 | 935,137 | 1,522,951 |
| 14 | 168,000 | 369,270 | 1,136,565 | 1,995,436 |
| 15 | 180,000 | 419,397 | 1,378,278 | 2,609,666 |

A number of people will say 15 years is too long. I don't have that much working time left or I cannot work at my present job for another 15 years. If you want more in less time, then you have to save more to begin with and make investments that have higher returns. That is why the best way to make money is as a business owner. We will look at that in more detail in the chapter on investments.

## HAVE TARGETS

It is important to add targets to your savings. Target how much to begin saving as a percentage of your income and target how much your savings should be per month within the next 3 months, 1 year, 3 years and so on. Don't be in a hurry to make quick money. Focus on being consistent with savings with the minimum amount of money you start with and keep growing this amount. Remember, saving is a habit for life. The reason for saving isn't because you are in a financial crisis; you will still need to keep saving even when you are a millionaire. Discipline yourself in regards to money and keep the promises you make to yourself. Remember the reasons why you are saving; to set yourself free to pursue your calling. Make sure you build relationships with people also. It is important because it is through relationships that you learn of opportunities to invest. It is these same people who become your clients, the buyers of the goods and services you produce.

Thomas, my other friend is now learning to readjust his expenses to set himself free from his dependence on salary. Unlike Raj, he didn't take his family for vacation; in fact he used his vacation days to help his wife set up a part time business. He has had to make painful choices in his life to find money to save. He moved his children to a cheaper school and is currently in the process of selling his house to pay off his mortgage and move to a cheaper rental. At age 41, Martin also experienced a wakeup call. He had two teenage children, qualifying for college in less than three years, consumer debt of over $50,000 and outstanding mortgage debt of over $250,000. He had no savings and no investments. He had a good job but he had been living from paycheck to paycheck for most of his adult life. In fact the more his income went up the faster his expenditures rose. His financial situation kept getting worse despite his better income. When the stress of living this way began to affect his marriage and his family, he decided to change. Together with his wife, a stay at home mum, they prioritized two things before anything else. First paying God, and then paying themselves. Before paying any of their expenses each month they paid themselves 10% of their income in the early months. They set a financial goal consisting of two objectives. The first objective was to be debt free in 3 years and the second was to build a passive income equivalent to his salary within 10 years. They scaled down their lifestyle and drastically reduced their expenses. Within 7 years Martin was debt free, had saved enough money for his children's university fees and set aside enough to build a passive income. Even though he did not leave his job, he felt that was where God had called him; he was no longer dependent on his paycheck. That set him free to enjoy the work he was doing without fear of job loss. After retiring from the job, Martin was able to move his family back to his native country, from the European country where he had worked to pursue the next stage in his call. To date he is still living off the passive income that he started building when he was 41 more than 20 years ago.

You have been working for over 10 years yet you do not have any savings? Maybe your children will be going to college soon and you do not have the money? Do you feel too old? You have many regrets? It's never too late. You can make a plan, set your goals and scale down your lifestyle and like Martin, you can set yourself free. It is even more urgent for you if you are older to implement the steps I outlined for you earlier. Start now.

## EXCUSES THAT KEEP YOU FROM SAVING

### EXCUSE #1. MY INCOME IS TOO SMALL OR MY EXPENSES ARE TOO MANY

If you live in the United States and make $500 per month, does that mean you cannot save? The question I would ask instead is, is it possible to move to a cheaper place? Even if you are married you can still scale your life back. There are seasons in life that require you to change your status and conserve money. It may even be disgraceful to you but you have to live with the inconvenience for the sake of starting to save. You must make it possible to start saving. It could be painful, but it will not be a permanent thing. Swallow your pride and suffer temporarily to build your future. Even if you can afford the lifestyle you have now, consider cutting back to build your future.

Are you and your spouse able to take up additional work? If you are married, plan with your spouse how, when and where to take up additional work. It is important not to sacrifice the time with your children as you seek additional income. If you are not married, but have children; seek ways to make additional income. Investigate what is in your area. Are there good day care centers that can help you look after your child as you take up additional work? Are there jobs that have day care centers? Do you have relatives you can seek help from to look after your children as you work more hours? Can you take up work remotely, such as online jobs? Can you do additional work from home? If you are single, maximize your time to take up additional jobs or work. All your new income should go towards your savings. Downgrade instead of upgrading your lifestyle. Remember it is only for a season, until you have reached your target financial goal and money is working for you.

You should make sure you have investments worth 2 or 3 times the rent for the house you are living in. If you are paying 300$ rent, you must ensure you have investments worth 1,000$ working for you now. You must understand in your mind why you are making the sacrifices you are and be deliberate about them, to build your future.

Luna and her husband Alex were both struggling with a small income from Alex's odd jobs in one of the states in the United States. His income was less than minimum wage and because they had two small children Luna could not afford to go out to work as that would require hiring a nanny which would cost more than the salary she could make. They had to move in with Luna's mother as they could not afford rent. They were in a dire financial situation as their income was not enough. Together they came up with a plan to raise their income. Alex took up additional work as a waiter and a security guard and at any given point he held at least three jobs. Luna had tried to set up to blog before but it wasn't generating any money. In one of the comments from her blog articles, a reader gave her an idea to begin online trainings on how to set up blogs and how to use social media to gain a following. The reader offered to be her first client. She took up the offer from the reader and gained other clients from more blog readers and followers on social media. Within a month she was making $500 from her online business and she was able to buy her own laptop and stopped relying on the desktop at her mother's house. Within 6 months she was able to generate $ 3,000 a month from her online training programs and within a year Alex quit his jobs to help her run the business and increase their income. They did not move out of their mother's house immediately but waited until they had saved enough money and eventually when they did, they decided to move to a lower cost state from where they could run their online business. This enables them to save on rent costs and the general cost of living. In Luna and Alex's case even though they had built an income of $3,000 monthly they waited until they had at least enough money to work for them to pay their rent. They also ensured it could pay their rent by moving to a cheaper state.

## EXCUSE #2. I AM IN DEBT

You can get out of debt and still save while at it. The first thing you should acknowledge if you are currently in debt is that your decisions put you in debt. Don't look at getting into more debt as a way out of your situation. Getting into debt was not a solution in the first place, even when it seemed like a quick solution. You have a utility bill to pay or your electricity will be cut off and it seems that the easiest way is to pay using a credit card and clear the credit card bill within a month. Unfortunately credit card debt piles up one bill at a time. Because you do not feel the pain of paying cash, it's easy to rack up credit card debt. It is not wise to borrow to pay expenses and liabilities. It's even worse when you are charged interest on debt to pay for things that are already taking away money from your pocket. You have to stop digging yourself into a hole. However there are circumstances where you can get into debt to gain asset. You must already have a portion of the money required to gain the asset.

Second, you have to take responsibility for your debt. Even if you got into debt because of some unlucky circumstances, the buck still stops with you. Do not blame others for being in debt. Even if the cause of your debt may be due to the failure of a business partner or a business deal gone badly, you still bear responsibility for your part in bringing about the debt. You must ensure you do due diligence or monitor your investments, so if there is any failure you still had a part to play in it. If you say you do not know how you got into debt, it indicates a level of disorder in your life. Before borrowing money, you must have several strategies of how you will repay the money. Never borrow money for expenses or to buy a liability. You may have good arguments as to why you are in debt, for example to take advantage of investment opportunities. If this is the case, ensure your return is 3 to 5 times the borrowed amount and make sure the maturity date of your investment is at least six months earlier than the due date for your debt repayment. Conduct due diligence to manage the risk of your investment. Your investment opportunity must have a level of certainty of gain. Otherwise you will be left struggling in debt.

Don't blame culture or tradition as the reason why you are in debt. A lot of people in the developed countries are in debt because of the use of credit cards. Credit cards are easily available and constantly advertised as a cheap way to pay your expenses. It's easy to say that you cannot live without a credit card or that you need credit card debt to build your credit history. In countries like the US where you need a credit card to build your credit history you can acquire prepaid cards that only allow you to spend what you have deposited in these cards. Another alternative is to use debit cards instead. Do not fall for that trap.

The next step is to evaluate how you got into debt. What wrong things have you believed about money and debt that you need to change? Do you have a problem of greed or bad judgment? Do you care more about people's opinion than you do your life? Look at your own internal arguments and reject them. Change your wrong mindset and wrong value system. Here are some points you need to look into:

1. **Make a list of all your creditors.** Find out which debt can be negotiated. Defer or extend loans that can be extended or deferred. Do not break relationship with your creditors and don't hide from them. If you owe an institution, negotiate with the decision makers about cancelling your interest and allowing you to only pay the principal. Being proactive about debt repayment will help you avoid situations where the institutions send debt collectors who sometimes use very unethical practices to collect debt.

2. **Prioritize debt owed to employees or subordinates.** Family relationships are easily killed by debt. Relationships are important; you need to settle family debt to uphold these relationships. If you owe money to any disenfranchised people; pensioners, the handicapped, poor people and orphans, pay them as fast as possible. God is the defender of the defenseless; if they hold anything against you then God is against you.

3. **Then, begin to pay off the debt with the highest interest.** The debt with the highest interest rate charged will increase the fastest. You need to stop the debt from increasing by clearing it as soon as possible. Do not spend more than 20% of your

income to pay off your debt. You still need to build your income sources to make it easier to pay the debt. Negotiate with your creditors to allow you to pay the principal first. The interest will then be charged on a reducing balance, reducing interest and debt load. People usually pay money to the creditors that put the most pressure on them. Do not do that, follow the above principles. If you pay the creditors who pressure you the most, you encourage other creditors to put pressure on you. Don't forget to celebrate your small victories. If you pay off one debt, take time to appreciate the victory, it motivates you. You are one step closer to freedom.

4. **Take the initiative to pay off your debt or at least to negotiate with your creditors.** Do not wait until they are looking for you, have a plan detailing your circumstances, when and how much you will pay them. Show your creditors the progress you are making towards paying their debt. This prevents pressure and attacks at you from the creditors. It also ensures you are the one in charge of the process. You do not want to give your creditors power over you, it can get very unpleasant.

5. **You can use a cheaper loan to offset high credit card debt such as a debt consolidation loan.** If you have credit card debt, get rid of your credit card and do not use it again once the loan is offset.

Martin had a consumer debt over $50,000 and teenage children waiting to go to college, and a mortgage loan on top of that. Once he set his goal to be debt free in three years, he began by taking 10% of the income left-over to pay his debts. He began by paying off his credit card debt. He was so consistent in paying off this debt that the credit card company wrote to him to grant him a waiver on the next repayment. Of course this is a trick by the credit card companies to ensure you only make minimum payments so they can keep earning interest off your loan.

About 25 years ago, a young man in Zimbabwe, Africa started his first business. Strive Masiyiwa, the young man took a bank loan using his family home as collateral to expand his business. He made a mistake taking a business loan against his home and failed to make the loan repayments and eventually fell behind on the debt. The bank repossessed his family home. He had to watch painfully as his wife and children lost their home and had to move out[22]. He was able to rise from that misfortune and today is one of the richest men in Zimbabwe with a net worth of $1.4 billion. You too can rise out of the misfortune of debt, your future awaits you, do not give up.

## EXCUSE #3, FAILURE TO PLAN

Many people do not save because they do not plan to save. Every month, you should have a goal of the amount to be set aside for saving. For people who are not married, take advantage of your singleness and save as much as possible now, even 80% of your income. For married people, you should strive to start and get to 30% of your net income quickly. You should agree with your spouse on how much to set aside each month. We will look at how to come up with a financial plan later on in this chapter. Always put God as number one. You do this through your tithes and offerings as discussed earlier.

I have noticed though even with my fellow church members that many people plan to save to buy unimportant things or meet family obligations that keep them further enslaved to their jobs. It is good to save towards your children's school fees but your goal must not end there otherwise you are still confined to your salary. Others like Raj save towards a vacation or buying a car or furniture and the like. My village mates save money for ceremonies and parties. Do not use your savings for frivolities. If you do not have the big picture as to why you are saving, you will keep using your savings to buy liabilities. Your financial goal is always to acquire assets towards setting yourself free and building your future.

## THE LITTLE FOXES; HIGH EXPENSE CULPRITS

**"Catch the foxes, the little foxes, before they ruin our vineyard in bloom".**
*(Song of Solomon 2:15)*

In a culture that relied heavily on agriculture, the author of this Bible verse gives us some wisdom. A farmer will tell you from experience - once your plants on the farm begin to bear fruit, wild animals, insects and other pests lie in wait to take the fruit. If you were a farmer you would lay traps to catch these pests. In the same way, as you begin to save if you do not catch the little things that are eating away your money, they will ruin your plan to save.

Usually simple decisions we make every day are responsible for our high expenses. When it comes to high expenditure, it is the small things such as consumer debt as it is called, that are largely responsible for debt and high expenses. I will list some of them:

1. **Consumer debt such as credit cards and auto loans are dangerous.** Consumer debt consists of loans towards meeting your expenses. If you keep using your credit card, you accumulate interest on your debt. If you only pay the minimum you will never pay off the debt. You end up paying high interest sometimes in excess of 30% per annum for years. Interest is not something you see unless you are looking for it. The statements come in such a way that you do not realize the amount of money you are paying in interest. The credit card companies encourage you to pay the minimum possible. Studies show most users underestimate how long it will take to repay credit card debt. If you have excessively high spending habits and are not disciplined, get rid of your credit card. In fact do not take a credit card. The risk of misusing a credit card particularly when you get unexpected expenses is too high.

2. **Auto loans are marketed to seem cheaper than they are.** Dealers do not tell you the total cost of the car you buy. They only talk about the monthly repayment to give the impression the car only costs the monthly amount. So if a car costs 25,000$, the dealer only talks about the $500 monthly repay-

ment. Once you add the interest charges and car insurance, the total cost of the car is upwards of $30,000. Buy used cars instead; find good used car dealers and car models that are most fuel efficient.

3. **Peer pressure, advertising and the pressure to have it all now are another trigger for spending.** We are living in a consumer driven culture and you have to be alert to the pressure to constantly spend money. Ask yourself before you spend money, do I really need this? Take a few days before buying something you want. If within the few days you are convinced you will die without it then you can buy it. America has some of the highest incomes in the world yet comparing the saving rate to GDP[23] countries like China, rank much higher in savings. America's consumer culture prevents them from saving.

As suggested earlier, track your expenses to find your expense culprits and deal with them.

4. **Impulse buying is another reason for high expenses.** Most people are likely to buy low price goods on impulse. High cost items like cars or houses are rarely bought on impulse because you would fill the pinch immediately. With low priced items you do not feel the costs unless you are tracking your expenditures. Avoid impulse buying by only carrying the exact cash. Shop owners try and make you buy items on impulse by displaying them in a way to appeal to you. Do not go shopping without a shopping list or while you are hungry. If you love shopping do not do

window shopping, it will only entice you. Plan your shopping trips.

5. **Household shopping** is also an area that can cause high expenses and therefore an area you can make savings gain. There is a big difference between purchasing items at bulk stores and ordinary stores. Investigate different stores that offer items in bulk and buy bulk to make those gains.

6. **Snacks and eating out** are other small expense items that can stack up to large expenses over time. See the calculations on potential savings on these small items and eliminate these expenses. Carry home cooked meals and plan your eating times to avoid eating out.

Your situation is unique to you; therefore you must learn your expenses and study your spending habits so that you can eliminate the small foxes that are eating your future.

## GUARANTEE SUCCESS IN SAVINGS

A number of people think that discipline is an incredible will power that is for the chosen few. The people who have attained high levels of spirituality, have denied themselves for long enough. The sheer number of books, articles and blogs on saving are a testament to the great desire out there to save. Yet if you spoke to the people around you now, your work colleagues, your family or your friends, you would realize that a vast number of them are struggling to consistently save money. We equate discipline in general to unnecessary suffering especially when we introduce budget and saving plans. Then we want to resist it.

If I could poll the readers, chances are high that I would find over 90% of you my readers are not hearing about the importance of savings for the first time through this book. You have heard about the need to save countless times. You may have been taught to save for a rainy day. You probably even have some money saved in a bank account, or as part of your pension plan. You have probably bought some sort of investment at one time or other. Yet for the most part, you still find that you are not disciplined enough to keep saving or you keep dipping into your savings to finance your lifestyle.

The idea of savings therefore carries a lot of guilt for a lot of people. It is a good thing, they know about it but somehow they cannot bring themselves to start saving, to be consistent or to keep saving. Life keeps interrupting them, when emergency requiring money occurs; they dip into their savings to resolve it. In a moment of weakness, they spend the money buying gadgets. Or they are cultured to believe, like most Europeans that savings are to be used for projects such as a vacation or a down payment for buying a house on mortgage. In my native country, women will typically form collective savings schemes, with a member being paid once a month. It is a good culture of saving among people who trust each other. The problem is amongst my tribesmen, the money they have spent years saving is used to hold parties and various ceremonies. What a waste!

Let me show you a way in which you can plan your saving to guarantee success. It will also debunk misconceptions surrounding saving. The process is called Financial Planning. Financial planning is a way to engineer your life starting from the result you want working your way backwards to the steps you need to take to get this result. You will understand that it does not require superhuman strength to start and keep saving. The goal of financial planning is to come up with a personal financial plan. A personal financial plan is a document to aid you in managing your money towards your goals. It gives you charge over your financial situation. If you are in a financial crisis, it means you have not been in charge of your finances for some time. A financial plan gives you back control of your money. A plan helps you avoid debt, set yourself free towards your purpose and to build your future. A financial plan governs three areas. How you spend money, savings and investment and your giving. You will need to keep reviewing your plan and ensure you stick to it to see the results you desire.

First, let us start with something that is seemingly unrelated. As mentioned earlier you were made for purpose. Your assignment on earth is to find and fulfill your purpose. Once you understand your calling, it begins to put into context your passions, your talents and your personality. The way you are, why you behave the way you do begins to make sense. Your purpose is in your uniqueness, your key to greatness. It is important to invest time and energy to discover your purpose so that you can begin to pursue it. I have written about how to discover your purpose in my book 'WHO AM I, WHY AM I HERE'. I encourage you to invest time to understand your WHAT before getting into your HOW.

After identifying your purpose, begin the financial

planning process with the end in mind. Look at your present situation in light of your purpose. Are you currently engaging in activities that lead you to or are part of your purpose? Do you require developing your gifts and talents into skills before you can generate income from them? Are you currently able to use your gifts and talents within your purpose and make a good enough income to meet your basic needs? Again, this process will require your time and energy but it's critical you do it before you determine savings. Do not be in a hurry to finish this chapter, it's not a novel. The benefit you will receive after reading this book is in how much of the principles here you can apply. You may need to read the chapters a few times before you grasp every-thing in it.

A financial plan will have timelines, dates by which you intend to have raised the target financial goals. The financial plan will show how much money you will need to have invested to generate an income which can support you and your family's basic needs. The plan should have timelines showing by when you expect to have a certain amount of investments generating enough money to support you monthly. Your targeted financial goals are always about building your future, the goal of your saving should not be to buy gadgets, pay for vaca-tions or even towards paying school fees. Ultimately your goal is to set yourself free from reliance on one income and to build multiple income sources in your future.

# STEPS TO CREATE A FINANCIAL PLAN

## STEP 1

Determine where you are. This step helps you **identify your current financial status**. By now you should have evaluated your expenses as earlier outlined in this chapter. You must identify your debt and be aware of your total income. I have outlined steps to identify your expenses, reduce your expense and repay your debt in the earlier paragraphs. If you have additional income other than your salary whether interest payments, dividend payment and other income, honorariums and part time allowances then total them up to determine your monthly income. Let's look at an example.

Jane Smith has a job she doesn't enjoy that pays her

$5,000 monthly. She evaluates her current status and lists her outstanding loans. She has outstanding student loans of $6,000. She is $3,000 in credit card debt and has an outstanding auto loan of $10,000. Her total current expenses are $4,800 monthly.

## STEP 2

How much will be require for you and your family to live on without relying on a salary? Come up with a strategy of how to get from where you are now to where you will be fulfilling your purpose. Make a plan of where to begin in pursuing your calling. Is it possible to make an income out of it? If it is possible, this would add to your income and increase how much you are saving monthly. Calculate how much you will need to be earning from your investments to meet your basic needs. Determine how much minimum passive income you will require and how much you may need as capital to start a business. Once you have a figure to work with, we can now begin to form financial goals to achieve the target passive income. This passive income allows you freedom to pursue your purpose.

**Develop your financial goals**. Once you know what your calling is and what your target investment amount is, develop financial goals around it. Set goals that free you to pursue your calling. These goals may include raising capital to start your business, building a passive income so you can leave your job and focus on your calling or building a certain amount in investments so you are not dependent only on your income.

In Jane's case, she would like to start her own financial consultancy. She has identified she will need investments of at least $300,000 generating at least $60,000 a year for her to leave her job and focus on building her business.

## STEP 3

**Make a plan of action to get to your goals**. Build a realistic plan on how you will get from where you are currently to the financial goals identified in STEP 2. Here you have to factor in your expenses and debt. In this step you should determine how much you need to save per month to attain your goals. Set timelines also indicating when you expect to reach your goal.

In our example Jane determines her priority expenses can be reduced to $3,000 including loan repayments. She makes a plan to sells off her car and offset her auto loan which will reduce her loan repayments. To build investments worth $300,000, she will need to free savings of $2,000 a month. She needs to invest the $24,000 at a rate of 30% per year to meet her goal in just over five years.

## STEP 4

**Implement the plan**. Finally you start the practical steps to achieve your goals. List all the things you need to do to free up the money you need to save. Cut out your expenses, sell cars or monetize them, open a saving account and set up instructions to send the money to your account each month. Think and strategize how to raise the required savings each month and also begin to look for investment avenues that will bring you the return you need to grow your money within the set timeline. Do your due diligence on investment opportunities that are available. Contact professional advisors and draw out contracts for your investments, agree on collateral and the like.

In this step, begin to do side businesses to increase the saved amount or take up additional jobs to increase your income and your savings.

Jane cuts down her expenses, sells her car and pays off the auto loan and begins to set aside the $2,000 every month in a saving account. She draws an agreement with a relative to invest in one of their businesses once she raises $10,000 for a share of the profit. She expects her share to give a return of 35% per year on her investment. She starts advertising for free online, her services to take up some freelance jobs.

## STEP 5

**Review and revise your plan often**. I recommend reviewing your plan at least yearly but you can review your financial plan as often as your circumstances change. If you move to a higher paying job for example, you can review your plan, your financial goals and your saving to reflect the higher income. Same thing if you get a bonus or some additional income. If you get children or get married or experience a health set back, review your plan to reflect the new circumstances. You may need to re-strategize in view of your changed situations.

In Jane's case, she has increased her savings to $3,000 within a year and is targeting to raise the savings even more by taking up more freelance work. She has built an additional income of $1,000 each month from part time jobs. She reviews her timelines downwards to 4 and a half years from 5 and a half years.

# ADDITIONAL SAVING TIPS

1. **Build your passive income**. Your financial goal may be to build passive income usually income from your investments. Passive income is an income that requires very little of your time to still make you money. Investments are a good source of passive income because they require little active involvement. You will only require time to track your investments and make sure they are performing and giving you the returns expected. Usually this would only take a few hours in a week or month depending on your type of investment. You do not have to wait until you have attained your target saved amount to start investing; begin to invest as soon as possible. Use the time it takes to acquire an investable amount to study investment opportunities, get financial education and do your due diligence. Seek out investment opportunities that are available to you through your network of friends, relatives and acquaintances.

2. **Summarize your financial goals into a statement** showing your target savings per month, target investments and realistic timelines. Stick the statement at a place of prominence, a mirror or on your refrigerator, so that it will motivate you to make sacrifices necessary towards building your future. Use your emotions, the desire to be free, to motivate you to save and keep saving. Keep referring to your financial plan often and communicate this plan clearly to your family so that they

are aware of why they are making the sacrifices they will need to make.

3. **Free yourself from dependence on your salary.** If you are working in an area you consider your purpose or that is leading you towards the fulfillment of your purpose, you will still need to free yourself from dependence on your salary. This will free you to not rely on your job and should you feel led to leave you can freely leave your job to start your own organization. Owners of successful businesses usually make more than employees ever make. Starting or running a business may not be a calling for everyone but you can still invest as an owner of a business through partnerships or buying shares. Set yourself free from the reliance on salary as soon as possible, have a target monthly savings based on the amount of investment that will build you your minimum monthly income.

4. **At all costs, avoid dipping into your savings**. Save your money in locked accounts or fixed deposit accounts where you have no access to the money. This will ensure you do not spend the money. Keep money out of your reach and avoid carrying more than you need to reduce your expenses. Keep track of your expenses by writing down your daily expenses. Review these expenses constantly, looking for opportunities to reduce them. Budget your income to fit only the basic expenses, so that you can stay within the budget. Once you have met your targeted financial goals and have money working for you, you can then

increase your lifestyle from the additional investment income.

Martin and his wife had set financial goals to be debt free in 3 years and build passive income in 10 years. From their financial planning their target was to eliminate $50,000 in consumer debt and sell off their house for $300,000 in 3 years. Their second target was to build passive income within 10 years by building investments worth $200,000. This was after factoring the education fees of $60,000 for their two children required within three years. Initially he was able to save only $1,000 a month after paying off his debt and while still making monthly mortgage payments. They were not able to sell their house immediately as the housing market was slow and they expected home prices to pick up in the coming years. They made drastic changes to their lifestyle. Within two years, Martin and his family were living on 60% of his income and setting aside the rest, more than $3,000 a month. This is how he paid off his consumer debt within the two years. On the third year they were able to sell their home at slightly less than $270,000 and pay off his mortgage and make initial payments towards his children's college fees. Within 7 years he had accumulated an additional $200,000 in investments.

In conclusion, no matter your circumstances whether you waited until your 40s or 50s to start saving or whether you are not making enough money, or you are simply unmotivated to save, there is something you can do to increase your savings and investments. The most important lesson in saving and investments is to focus your activities towards your goals and your purpose. The reason you save is so that you have the financial freedom to pursue your areas of interest without having to work simply for money. In the next chapter we would add another tool, budgeting to be used to ensure success in paying yourself. I will simplify the process even for the most technically averse reader. In the end, you must understand WHY you are saving; this is the key behind your success in saving.

# PRINCIPLES OF SAVING SUCCESS

1. Get a strong reason to start. The strongest reason to save money is to free you to pursue your purpose. Identify your calling. Break it down into actionable steps and include the steps in a financial plan. Look at your plan often. This will provide the fuel you need to pay yourself and build a secured financial future.

2. Take responsibility for your financial state and set about to redeem wasted time. Develop an abundance mindset. Believe it is possible to come out from lack, poverty or financial crisis.

3. Don't use your savings to buy liabilities or to pay for your expenses. If you need to set aside money for future school fees for your children, make a plan towards it and invest the money depending on your time frame.

4. Invest in knowledge. Spend a fixed amount of time daily developing yourself in your area of calling. Develop your gifts and talents, improve your skills and gain experience in your area.

5. Environment. Surround yourself with people

who will propel you to succeed and fulfill your purpose. Get biographies and teachings from people who have succeeded in gaining financial freedom and people who are leaders in your area of interest.

6. Pay yourself after paying God, by saving and investing money. Build your assets. Do not pay your expenses first. Do not pay monthly shortfalls with your savings. Let your mind come up with ways of making more money to pay your bills. Build your financial intelligence to solve financial shortfalls.

7. Keep your expenses low. Only spend on necessities, you can buy luxuries with profit from your assets later. Find money to invest. Find ways to save money, spend money only on what you need. Look for ways to increase your income by developing your skill; take up part time work and use your skills to get an increase in income.

8. Don't get into debt. If you are already in debt, make a plan and pay off your debts. Pay off the most expensive debt as soon as possible. Do not borrow to eat. Only take loans to purchase assets, things that will add money to your pockets. If it will not bring additional income, do not take out the loan.

9. Develop a personal financial plan and set time bound goals. Use your financial plan to determine how much you need to have saved and invested, and by when. Target to save as much as possibl.

10. Begin to save immediately. The goal of savings is

to invest. Convert your savings into investments as soon as possible so that your money can begin to work for you.

# GOLDEN NUGGETS

- Bills and expenses are one of the key tools used by Satan to control people

- If you are paying 50 to 70% of your income towards meeting your bills, you are a slave to those bills.

- If you are married, make sure you begin the process together with your spouse so that you are on the same page about your finances and the changes to be made.

- Don't rush to pay your expenses, stretch out your payments. Defer expenses that can be paid later.

- Make sure you build relationships with people. It is important because it is through relationships that you learn of opportunities to invest.

- There are circumstances where you can get into debt to gain asset. You must already have a portion of the money required to gain the asset.

- Conduct due diligence to manage the risk of your investment. Your investment opportunity must have a level of certainty of gain. Otherwise you will be left struggling in debt.

- Your financial goal is always to acquire assets towards setting yourself free and building your future.

- You must learn your expenses and study your

spending habits so that you can eliminate the small foxes that are eating your future.

- A personal financial plan is a document to aid you in managing your money towards your goals. It gives you charge over your financial situation.

- It is important to invest time and energy to discover your purpose so that you can begin to pursue it.

- Your targeted financial goals are always about building your future, the goal of your saving should not be to buy gadgets, pay for vacations or even towards paying school fees.

# CHAPTER 4
# BUDGETING

*"A budget is telling your money where to go instead of wondering where it went." John C. Maxwell.*

In this quote John Maxwell reveals an important principle behind a budget. Without a plan of how to spend money, you are bound to struggle to manage it well.

As we saw previously, a financial plan is important to guarantee your success in saving. It is the key to acquiring the discipline in saving, where many have failed before. Once you have your financial plan, the budget should stem out of your financial plan. Budget is a plan of allocating your expenses according to your income. Having determined how much you want to save per month after creating your financial plan, come up with a budget. Out of your income allocate money to your basic expenses in terms of percentage of income. This is the essence of the budget. A budget also helps you keep track of your expenses each month and to determine on a month to month basis, what areas need to be cut back and what areas need more money. It helps you make deliberate decisions on allocation of money, eliminate waste and impulse buying.

## DISCIPLINE TO FOLLOW THE BUDGET

Just as a financial plan gives you control of your money,

a budget is the tool that helps you implement your plan. With is a budget? You choose what will happen to your money and when.

The budget is also important as a tool to communicate with your family. You will need to cut down your expenses drastically to meet your financial goals. The budget will help explain to the family how you will all go about meeting these financial goals. If you are married, ensure you do the financial plan and the budget with your spouse so that you are on the same page about your finances. Once both of you are in agreement, communicate with your children as they will also need to scale back on their lifestyle. Explain your action in a way your children will understand according to their age. Every family member should know what is expected of them and the limits they have when it comes to money. The children will need to understand why they will not be getting gifts, new toys and gadgets any more. They will also have to understand why their allowance will be cut or completely eliminated so that they are all on board and can help you to implement the changes needed. Work out ways to reward each other for sticking to the budget. These rewards do not need to be financial; it could be just extra time on things the children like to do. These may include extra time playing their favorite games, cooking their favorite meals for them, spending quality time with them and taking them out to the park and so on.

Transfer your savings amount automatically to a savings account or a money market fund[i] that is hard to access. This account should not have a debit card. Use a mobile application in case you have a smartphone to keep

i    Explained in Chapter 8

track of your expenses. Alternatively you can download a template in Excel sheets to track your expenses. Make sure your expenses are within the budget. Once you exhaust the allocated budget per item, do not spend any more money on that item. Do all your shopping once a month in bulk and do not enter a shopping mall after that. Keep only the cash that you require in a day, do not carry more than the cash you require per day. Cut up your credit cards. Do not carry your debit cards unless you are going shopping. Carry a shopping list consisting only of items that you absolutely need. Do not go with your friends for shopping particularly if you do not know how to say no to them. Sell your car if you can use public transport. Consider exchanging your car for a more fuel efficient car. Get a fuel card and use it.

After a month of tracking your expenses, look at your expenses again and cut out or reduce expenses. You will discover there are items you may not have originally seen when doing your priority expenses earlier that you can now do without. A budget will uncover hidden expenses, fees and lost interest paid to others that can be eliminated. Once identified, all unnecessary expenses should be cut. All savings made should be added to your target savings goal and put in your savings account. Review your budget to eliminate waste and keep reviewing it each month until you are satisfied that your expenses are on basic needs only.

# BUDGETING PROCESS

### 1. Setting goals
The budget should align with your financial goals set in chapter 3. If your target savings per month is $2,000, set

a budget that allows you to find that money by reducing your expenses. If you exceed your target savings, set new target savings goals. The additional savings will be used to reduce your timelines so that you meet your target financial goals earlier.

### 2. Making lifestyle decisions

A budget is critical to understanding what changes will be made to your lifestyle. If your rent budget has to go down, you have to move to a cheaper house to stay within the budget. Be realistic when setting the budget to make it easier to implement.

### 3. Expense Tracker

You may need to track your expenses for at least a month to uncover hidden expenses and wastes. You can write your expenses down daily on paper or you can use computer software or mobile applications available for tracking expenses. A lot of money is wasted on the smaller items because they are harder to remember. You can never forget how much you spend monthly on your rent, but it may be hard to know how much you are spending on small items such as snacks and drinks. Having your expenses written down helps you identify hidden expense items. Make sure you also note any additional income that comes in monthly.

### 4. Forecast future needs

It is important to anticipate any future needs and to plan for them. If you expect a new baby in your family, factor that in the budget and plan for how to adjust for new expenses on diapers and baby food and so on. If you are expecting a raise at work, factor it in your budget and use all your additional income to add to your savings. You may need school fees for yourself or your children in future, budget for that also by setting aside small amounts every month towards this.

### 5. Implementing the budget

Start with the big items first. Pay your tithes and offerings first, then pay yourself and for your personal development. After that, pay the priority items when they fall due. You should have automatic instructions sent to your bank to pay tithes, offerings and savings as soon as the money hits your account. Big ticket items such as rent, loan repayments should then be made from your account. Any additional income that comes to your account such as bonuses, allowances, investment income should all be sent to your savings account as soon as it clears into your account.

### 6. Controlling your spending

Do everything within your power to cut your expense to priority items only. Keep reminding yourself and your family why you are doing what you are doing and keep your financial goals in prominent view so that the whole family knows where you are going. If the goal is to have $500,000 in investments in 3 years, let every family member be aware and know their role. I have suggested things you could do to cut back your expenses drastically.

### 7. Evaluating your performance

Every month, compare your expenses according to your expense tracker or the written down expenses and the budget. Make sure your expenses are within the budget. Keep a monthly review of your budget versus your actual expenditure and tighten controls to ensure you are strictly following the budget.

# SAMPLE RECOMMENDED BUDGET

| ITEM | PERCE-NTAGE OF INCOME | BUDGET ALLO-CATION | ACTUAL AMOUNT USED |
|---|---|---|---|
| Tithes and Offering | 15% | | |
| Savings | 10%-30% | | |
| Emergency fund<br>Self education fees<br>Investment | | | |
| Housing | 15% | | |
| Rent or mortgage repayment<br>Home insurance<br>Land rates and property taxes<br>Repairs, maintenance, home improvements if you own it | | | |
| Utilities | 5% | | |
| Water, Electricity and Gas<br>Mobile phone airtime/phone<br>Internet bundles/broadband | | | |
| Family expenses | 15% | | |
| School fees<br>School supplies<br>Childcare<br>Children's Clothing<br>Family giving | | | |

| | | | |
|---|---|---|---|
| Transport | 5% | | |
| Public transport<br>Car loan repayment<br>Fuel<br>Car insurance<br>Car maintenance | | | |
| Personal care | 5% | | |
| Grooming & beauty | | | |
| Insurance | 5% | | |
| Life insurance | | | |
| Medical<br>Health insurance<br>Out of pocket doctor bills/medication<br>Dental/optical | | | |
| Household supplies and groceries | 10% | | |
| Household shopping<br>Groceries and Eating out expenses | | | |
| Debt | Up to 20% | | |
| Student loan<br>Other loan<br>Car loan | | | |

What are some of the things Martin, from the earlier example and his family did to ensure they were debt free and could live on a passive income within seven years? After setting their financial goals and building a financial plan Martin sat down with his wife and children and came up with the budget together. They agreed with the children that they could only get new clothes and shoes once a year. The only exception is if they outgrew their shoes. They decided to cut out holidays altogether including trips home to his native country. They were able to reduce their food expenses by buying bulk and avoiding unnecessary snacks. Reducing their food intake overall was also one of the things that helped them bring down the food budget costs. They cut down driving and Martin was able to reduce his fuel expenses by only using the car for necessary trips. Once they sold their house they were able to move to a cheaper house in a safe and friendly neighborhood.

# CASH FLOW ANALYSIS

Cash Flow analysis is the tracking of monthly income compared to expenses. It gives an overview of the whole year. This analysis helps you to plan your income and anticipate your expenses or reduce your expenses. You can evaluate your progress yearly when doing your financial plan review. This is useful for three categories of people:

1. Those who do not have fixed incomes or those who are already receiving additional income that is not regular. Such additional incomes include investment income, allowances, bonuses and interest. As you build your savings and investments, the additional income you receive should begin to go up. Your cash flow analysis will give you a picture of your investment income growth progress. A number people do not have a fixed salary, either they generate commissions or they have businesses and rely on income gained from such businesses. It is important to track you

income so as to plan out your months depending on income peaks and low seasons. Endeavor to keep your expenses as low as possible and use the savings each month to build a passive income.

2. Those who identify opportunities to reduce their expenses gradually. Some expenses may require time to reduce because of the process it takes to scale down living standards. For example it may take a month or two to reduce rent expenses, sell off cars and eliminate car insurance and maintenance. Other expenses such as debt may take time to eliminate, but once cleared will reduce expenses significantly. A cash flow analysis helps you to track monthly your progress in reducing expenses.

3. Those who have a lot of periodic expenses. There are expenses that are not monthly such as college or school fees. A cash flow statement will show the fluctuations in expenses. Annual expenses such as insurance costs will also cause monthly expenses to differ. If you do bulk shopping on some household items your expenses may be reduced from monthly to quarterly expenses.

## SAMPLE CASH FLOW PLAN

### Irregular income and expenses

| MONTH | TOTAL INCOME | TOTAL EXPENSE | MORE SAVINGS |
|---|---|---|---|
| JANUARY | 5,000 | 6,000 | -1,000 |
| FEBRUARY | 3,000 | 2,000 | 1,000 |
| MARCH | 6,000 | 4,000 | 2,000 |

| APRIL | 5,000 | 2,000 | 3,000 |
|-----------|--------|--------|--------|
| MAY | 6,000 | 3,000 | 3,000 |
| JUNE | 4,000 | 3,000 | 1,000 |
| JULY | 3,000 | 2,000 | 1,000 |
| AUGUST | 4,000 | 2,000 | 2,000 |
| SEPTEMBER | 4,000 | 3,000 | 1,000 |
| OCTOBER | 3,500 | 3,000 | 500 |
| NOVEMBER | 2,500 | 2,000 | 500 |
| DECEMBER | 5,000 | 4,000 | 1,000 |
| **TOTAL** | **51,000** | **36,000** | **15,000** |

# BUDGET ALLOCATIONS

Every individual is unique and every family has its own unique needs. There are some general guidelines; however that helps in the budget process. These are the recommended allocations depending on your responsibilities. It is important to note that these are general guides and may not custom fit everyone. It is important to work out your own allocations based on your family or individual circumstances and your financial goals.

For those who are married and or have children, the recommended allocation is 20/30/50. At least 20% of your income should go towards family giving, tithes and offering. Tithes would take up 10%, offerings 5% and family giving would also be 5%. You may choose to invest on behalf of your family, but depending on your circumstances. If you support any parents or siblings, you have to plan how to provide this support whether monthly or one off lump sum. Target to save 30% of your income but you should begin with at least 10%. Your total priority expenses should not exceed 50%. If your expenses currently exceed this, work your way down to 50% and save the rest.

If you are in debt, the recommended allocation is 20/10/20/50. At least 20% of your income should be for tithes, offering and other giving. Save at least 10% of your income. Use up to 20% of your income to offset your debts. Once these are cleared move this percentage to increase your savings to 30%. Ensure that your priority expenses do not exceed 50%.

Those who are single and do not have children or dependants should take advantage of their reduced responsibilities to save. The recommended allocation is 20/50/30. The 20% of your income goes to tithes, offerings and other giving. Your target savings is 50% of your income. Your priority expenses should not exceed 30% of your income. This way you are able to prepare yourself for responsibilities ahead if you get married and have children.

As we have seen, the budget is a tool to use towards ensuring your success in paying yourself. The budget must come from your financial plan and must be made to suit your unique situation. You can keep adjusting it according to your changing circumstances including changes in income, expenses and anticipated expenses. Ultimately, for you to succeed at paying yourself you have to master the laws of money. What we have covered so far in budgeting is the administration of money which is an important law of money. Anything you do not control by administrating well will control you. We will look at more laws governing money in the next chapter. It is important to remember the following budget pointers.

# BUDGET POINTERS

1. Set your budget according to your financial goal.
2. Track your expenses and make it a habit to cut out unnecessary expenses regularly.
3. Ensure you stay within the budget.
4. Keep reviewing your budget and your cash flow analysis for saving opportunities.

# GOLDEN NUGGETS

- Just as a financial plan gives you control of your money, a budget is the tool that helps you implement your plan.

- Transfer your savings amount automatically to a savings account or a money market fund that is hard to access.

- Review your budget to eliminate waste and keep reviewing it each month until you are satisfied that your expenses are on basic needs only.

- A cash flow analysis helps you to track monthly your progress in reducing expenses.

- Ensure that your priority expenses do not exceed 50%.

- Anything you do not control by administrating well will control you.

# CHAPTER 5

# MASTER THE LAWS OF MONEY

*It doesn't matter how much you make, as long as you are ignorant of the laws of money, you will never be rich!*

In the previous chapter we covered important ways of administrating your money through budgeting. We saw that a budget is a plan on how to spend your money and if you do not have one, you are more likely to spend your money without realizing where it is going. We look at an example below that debunks the myth most people hold; that once you earn a lot of money, you are rich. The results show that you can only be rich by mastering the laws of money.

## WHY HIGH INCOME EARNERS ARE STILL BROKE

In the 2009 Sports Illustrated article on *how and why athletes* go broke quoted earlier, it is reported that major professional athletes have a penchant for losing money. The reasons for this and why they are in financial distress or bankrupt a few short years after retirement is because they are ignorant of money and violate the laws of money. One major NFL player earned 18 to 20 million dollars in salary alone, over a period of 12 years.

He admits to having lost several million dollars out of *total ignorance*'. He made a series of poor investment decisions due to ignorance on money and investing. Players as young as 18 years old join professional sports leagues in the United States. A lot of these athletes are like lottery winners. They come from poor or average backgrounds into a lot of money suddenly, but with little or no financial education. Many such athletes live high and expensive lifestyles while they make millions not realizing the millions they make are supposed to last them a lifetime. Once they retire, they cannot continue their lifestyles and end up broke or bankrupt. One of the rare exceptions was the legendary American basketball player Magic Johnson. He invested while still a professional basketball player in a chain of movie theatres in low income neighborhoods. Over the course of his career and after retirement, he diligently built Magic Johnson Enterprises which has partnerships with various profitable companies such as Starbucks and Best buys. Magic Johnson Enterprises has invested over a billion dollars in various communities. Magic began by admitting his ignorance. He did not know anything about business and he sought expertise from professionals to learn about money.

## BREAKING FROM FINANCIAL DISTRESS.

Many of you reading this book are in financial distress or are bound to your salary. How do you break away from this? Admit you don't know. The first rule of problem solving is always to admit you have a problem. Humble yourself and acknowledge that you are ignorant of the laws of money. You need to do a critical evaluation of yourself and your knowledge of the laws of money. The lack of knowledge on the principles of money makes us to suffer pain in our finances. We fail to use money to our advantage out of ignorance on how money works. You have to determine to eliminate your ignorance on the laws of money. You have to understand the laws of money and how to use them to your advantage.

Once you have identified where your problem lies, look for teachings and books on financial liberty and empowerment. I have a powerful book I have written about money: MONEY WON'T MAKE YOU RICH. Educate yourself on the laws of money. Find mentors who can teach you, people who have developed financial independence. In the age of the internet, you do not need to know these people personally or see them. You can find as much material on these people as possible on the internet. Investigate their lives, read their biographies, watch their interviews and documentaries about them. Find out the principles they used to get where they are and apply them diligently.

Unlearn false teachings on money that are responsible for where you currently find yourself. We have been taught falsely that being good will bring you money. The current church, particularly the charismatic church is teaching a lot of falsities about money, particularly the principle of giving. Giving alone will not bring money. People have been taught about *sowing a seed* in relation to giving money in church or to a certain pastor. However as we have seen earlier, that is not the definition of sowing seeds. This doctrine has been used to manipulate and exploit many in the church until there is a callousness now attached to giving. Pastors and ministers of the gospel have used the church as an avenue to enrich themselves. The prosperity gospel has produced many millionaire pastors while their congregants languish in poverty. Another false doctrine taught by the church is that prayer and fasting will result in riches. Churches particularly in Africa regularly hold breakthrough conferences, meetings to pray and fast for financial breakthrough. People are constantly flocking to church to receive deliverance out of poverty, to have the spirit of poverty cast out of them. The church is in such a state of ignorance when it comes to money. Other teachings exist which keep people ignorant about money. Hard work at your job alone will not make you rich. People spend countless hours at their jobs, increasing their skills, studying, working hard only to retire and live on peanuts. Even when they succeed at making more money, if they do not learn the laws of money they will not become financially independent. Learn all the laws of money and apply them consistently together with other general laws, until you have gained mastery.

# PRINCIPLES OF MONEY

## RETENTION

The first law of money is retention. Money is not for spending. Money is not meant to be spent, money must be retained. Money is a seed for money; if you do not plant money you do not harvest money. As long as you do not have money working for you, you have to be frugal. Ensure you only spend money on what you need. We have seen ways of how to create budgets and ensure you live within them. You have to pay yourself to be able to have money working for you. If you don't set aside money for yourself, you are trapped in financial crisis and failure, no matter how much you make a secured financial future will only be a dream.

The problem with the consumer culture is that it glorifies spending and vilifies frugality. The effects of this culture are felt across the world and across different income levels. They are a great equalizer. In South Africa, 70% of high income earners with annual income above $70,000 had no savings while 14% struggle to make ends meet . Despite rising individual earnings, many are living beyond their means due to reckless spending and inability to accept a mindset change, the study found. The discipline of saving is not inherited, it must be acquired. So whereas the older generations of Africans born and raised in the 1950s and 1960s grew up with great financial difficulties and out of those struggles learnt the value of money and this law of money, the new generation born in the 1980s,1990s and 2000s do not espouse those values. Africa is the fastest growing consumer market in the world. This has been attributed to the rising middle class who are spending their money extravagantly. Average savings rate in various African countries are low but in the last 40 years have dropped even further even with increased access to financial services particularly in rural areas. In Kenya the savings rate has dropped from 25% of GDP in 1974 to 11% in 2014. In Malawi the drop was from 20% to 14%, in Rwanda the savings rate dropped from 20% to 14% and South Africa's savings rate dropped from 28% to 15% of GDP[25]. There has been a shift in generational thinking, from conservative spending to the embrace of the prodigious lifestyle among those in Sub Saharan Africa. It is not just enough for Africans to come out of poverty, and indeed the world, they must learn the law of retention.

On the other hand, the People's Republic of China has the highest savings rate in the world. Estimates put savings at 30% to 50% of GDP in 2015. Chinese savings have bought large amounts of United States government bonds; China is the largest investor of U.S government bonds in the world. What are the reasons people in China save more than the rest of the world? The one-child policy means that they have fewer family expenses and they can save more. This is combined with a frugal culture prevalent in most of China. The consumer habits have eroded some of this practice in major cities; savings rate for rural households is much higher than in urban homes even though the income is lower in rural homes. The uncertainty of the incomes for these rural homes, mainly from farming makes them save more for emergencies. Cultural practice among Chinese dictates that the children take care of their parents as they grow old. With the advent of the one-child policy, older people cannot rely on their child to look after them in future so they put away a lot of their income to cater for retirement. In fact, Chinese people between 40 to 65 years of age are responsible for most of the savings.

This law, that money is not to be spent is what Martin used to set himself free from debt and build investment income. My friend Raj however still believes he has a right to spend money as long as he is making it. He is violating the law of retention. These two men are now worlds apart financially. One is fully dependent on his income and the other lives off his investment income yet they both have similar lifestyles. Martin however has freedom to do as he likes and is not bound to his job. Raj, on the other hand will have to keep working at the current rate or harder to sustain his lifestyle.

# MULTIPLICATION

The second law of money is multiplication. Once you have retained your money. You have to begin by paying yourself. Set aside money in form of savings, earning you at least a little interest. The master in the parable of the talents challenges the wicked and lazy servant. He should at least have saved the money with bankers for some interest. This is the basic starting point. However you have to ensure you do not remain at the beginning. Study and look for opportunities to multiply the money even more through investing. The other servants were able to multiply their talents by 100% in the time they were given. Seek to multiply your savings through investments. To be able to reach the level of making money work for you, you have to succeed at retaining money, be diligent concerning money and multiply money through investments. In other words, money is to be administered, if you do not control money by administrating it properly, it will control you instead. We will look at investment options in the chapters to come.

Julia, another member of my church, was working as a school teacher and was married with 8 children. She started attending my training sessions where I taught these principles and she took them and began to turn her life around. She had the responsibility of looking after her 8 children. Despite having many bills and expenses because of her large family, she set aside money to set up her own business. Although her first business did not work she learnt the lessons and decided to try again. Eventually she succeeded in building businesses that span 5 countries with over 500 people working for her. As she built her businesses she did not just focus on making more money only but also improving herself and her services. She went back to school and got her master's degree and then her PHD and was able to move to a more engaging job within the government administration. She does not depend on her salary to support her family and she has financed 5 children in the university from the proceeds from her businesses.

## DILIGENCE

The third law of money is diligence. When we talk about diligence we equate it to working hard. Whether physically working hard or working hard at your job, diligence is always restricted within the confines of work or employment. Some of the hardest working people in the world are poor. People who use physical labor such as rice farmers in China or market transporters in Africa put in hours in rice fields or pulling carts to and from markets and so on. Why aren't they rich? Yet billionaires like Bill gates or Mark Zuckerberg do not spend hours in farm fields or market streets laboring physically. Diligence is therefore not necessarily hard work.

According to Webster's dictionary *diligence is constant effort to accomplish what is undertaken; exertion of body or mind without unnecessary delay or sloth; due attention; industry; assiduity.*

Diligence is not just the use of the body, neither is it

just within the confines of a job but diligence is constant effort to accomplish any undertaking. It includes exerting your mind in thought, in creativity and ideas. Therefore diligence as far as money is concerned is an exerted effort to learn all there is to know about money or to employ knowledge through use of professionals. It means you have to devote time to understand your own financial situation, how you spend money, where you spend money. Learn how you earn money, where you earn money and how to increase how much you are earning from your job or profession. Learn and apply knowledge on how to create money and opportunities around you that can help you create money. Financial intelligence is the ability to spot opportunities to create money. Financial intelligence is being creative and coming up with various ideas to solve financial problems. It is a skill that can be learnt and mastered.

Financial intelligence is made up of certain traits:

1. **Financial literacy.** This is the ability to read and understand numbers that surround money. It includes the ability to create, read and understand budgets, financial plans, and financial statements and use them to your advantage.

2. **Investment strategies.** This is the science of making money. Investment strategies are plans on making money work for you. Investment strategies make the difference between making money and losing money. Becoming proficient at investing requires that you learn how to find investment opportunities and how to evaluate this opportunities realistically and determine how much risk is involved in such an investment.

It is important also to know how to raise money to take advantage of these opportunities without necessarily borrowing from a bank. You also need to know how to use specialized knowledge available around you. How to use accountants, lawyers, appraisers, real estate agents, advertisers and the like in your investments.

3. **The law.** You need to understand the law governing your country. This allows you to take advantage of legal loopholes to make or save money. In such a way that is used constantly in tax avoidance. Tax avoidance is a legal way that companies use to reduce how much tax they pay. Another way to use the law is using corporations, companies and trusts as investment vehicles to reduce tax on investment incomes. While an individual can make investments, there are certain advantages that companies have when it comes to investments that are not available to individuals.

## MONEY MAKING

The fourth law of money is that money is created. Out of diligence, we can learn how to create money in two ways. The first way money is created and most common way is by exchanging time for money. Majority of the world's population exchange their time for money from the employer. One can still exchange their time but instead to create goods and services which they then exchange with their employer. This ensures higher pay for the individual. For example because doctors and engineers have developed their skills and talents more they are able to create services with those skills which they then exchange within the organizations they work for and receive a better income. People who have low skills and little differentiation in their services end up making minimum wage. Cleaners for example are mostly paid minimum wage because almost anyone can learn to clean within a very short time, hours maybe, minutes even. However it takes a lot of time and effort to learn to be a neurosurgeon, therefore the income is higher for them. You must learn and differentiate yourself in your knowledge, skill and experience. The more unique and relevant your solutions, the more money you command. Read every day, develop yourself and increase your knowledge and wisdom about your call and areas of interest.

Olga joined our church seven years ago. She was a divorcee and in the separation process she had lost everything including her job. She had a young child and out of desperation she decided to join the church. From learning this principle she discovered an opportunity to change her life. She became proactive towards her goal and set up her own business training the youth, an area she was passionate about. After a year she began to get recognition from the authorities in her city and was invited to join the youth parliament. Her model; training the youth had succeeded and she started to expand it. During the 2008 financial crisis which affected Ukraine badly, she fell behind on her mortgage payments and the bank took her to court. In the process she saw an opportunity to represent herself and others by going back to school and training as a lawyer. While in law school, she was invited to join a parliamentary committee enacting laws on banking and mortgage debt. She got an opportunity to work and learn from experienced lawyers. Once she became a lawyer she was able to advocate for others and from her good work, she was invited to be a media consultant appearing frequently in various popular television stations. Now, she was not just making a living but she was now giving life to others through her work.

Dr. Ben Carson was born in southwest Detroit, Michigan to a mother who was one of 24 children with just third grade education. Ben's mother, Sonya got married at age 13 and had her first child at age 20. When Ben was 8, his parents divorced and Ben and his older brother were raised by their mother. Sonya worked two to three menial jobs at a time caring for children and cleaning houses. She worked very hard and long hours and this shaped how Ben viewed poverty. By fifth grade though, Ben was the class' worst student. An eye test revealed he had poor vision and his school gave him free glasses. From that point on he became a voracious reader and loved science and math. After high school he proceeded to Yale University and graduated with a major in psychology. He worked throughout the college during summer breaks. He got a job during one such break at a motor company in Michigan and for two years worked as a highway cleanup crew, and then he worked at a production plant for another motor company. He then enrolled in the medical school, University of Michigan Medical School through a scholarship. He did his medical residency and became a neurosurgeon. He retired from active practice and ran for the US presidential elections in 2015-2016 until he withdrew his candidacy. As Ben Carson increased in knowledge and skills his income kept growing until eventually he became world renown for his skills as a neurosurgeon.

The second way to create money is as a business owner. You do not need to open and run a business to be one. You can be a business owner by holding shares of a company and investing in shares listed in public stock exchanges. You have to learn to find investment opportunities and business opportunities. Opportunities to make money are taken advantage of by business owners. In a business, employees make the least money, only a small fraction of what they make for the business, usually this amount is less than 10%. The income the employee makes is guaranteed and fixed because the employee does not bear any risk in the business, they do not share in the rewards other than performance bonuses that they may receive. Business owners however take the bulk of the profits that a business makes. Depending on the structure of the business, an owner does not have to spend time in the business. They do not exchange their time for the income. The highest reward goes to those who are able to create goods and services that have great demand because they meet needs. The best business for you to invest in is investing in yourself. The last decade has seen many billionaires and millionaires made out of the businesses they founded. Their products were widely accepted, some such as Facebook becoming among the wealthiest companies in the world and their owners among the wealthiest people in the world.

A teacher working in a developing country earning about $200 dollars a month was able to save $30 in the first two months that he began saving. That is less than 10% of his income per month. With the $30 he invested in his wife who was a housewife. Using this money, the wife bought a small charcoal grill, a frying pan, cooking oil, salt and some wheat floor. She would wake up at 4 am each morning and make different snacks. She would pack them and go with her husband to the school and by 11 am each weekday she had sold all her snacks. Within a week she was able to turn a small investment of $30 to $100. In 2 months her small capital had grown to $500 dollars and she could now look at expanding the business.

In 1976 one college dropout and two partners started a business out of one of the parents' garage. Together they sold what they had and raised $1,350 to fond the business. Apple Computers was formed. A year later, two investors put in $92,000 in cash and secured a loan for the company of $250,000. At the public listing of Apple shares in the New York Stock Exchange, in December of 1980, the founders Steve Jobs and Stephen Wozniak had 7.5 Million shares and 4 Million shares worth $217 Million and $116 Million dollars respectively. One of the investors Mike Markkula had 7 million shares worth $250 Million dollars. Today Apple is now worth almost $1trillion.

Other laws help your abilities around money. Money is a terrible master but a good slave. Money is to be mastered. The law of restraint helps you learn to direct money. Money should not determine your mood. If money determines whether you are sad or happy then money controls you. You have to teach yourself to exercise control over money. A practical way to do this is to see how long you can go after receiving your income without spending your money. Check yourself, how do you feel when you do not have money, are you unable to sleep? Are you filled with worry? Can you go about your day without spending money or spending only the minimum you need to survive? Exercise yourself in restraint; never obey the dictates of money. One of the fruits of the Holy Spirit is self-control. Now we all know fruit is grown, it is not just given. Grow in character; self-control, love, patience and kindness, understanding, knowledge and wisdom. Become wealthy inside before getting money. People who do not know how to get money do either of two things. They spend money unwisely ending up worse than they were or two they become hoarders because they do not know how to replace the money should they spend it. Build your internal wealth, the wealth of soul and spirit so that your reliance is not on the money, money will just be a tool for you. Exercise yourself in self-control. We will learn how to control your appetite in the chapter titled the same.

# ROAD TO MASTERY

1. Educate yourself out of the ignorance surrounding money.
2. Determine to learn the laws of money and apply them consistently until you gain mastery. Life takes away from those who don't have and don't do anything with what they have and gives to those who have done something with what they have. You must be radical about your commitment to the laws of money.
3. Learn financial intelligence and create money as an owner not as an employee, even if you are employed. Exploit your talents and abilities to

create more value for you.

4. Control money, do not become a slave of money. Examine yourself, your motives. Set yourself free from the dictates to money. Tell money what to do, do not have money telling you what to do. Do not seek your identity in money or try to find happiness in money. That is equivalent to chasing shadows.

# GOLDEN NUGGETS

- You have to determine to eliminate your ignorance on the laws of money.

- Unlearn false teachings on money that are responsible for where you currently find yourself.

- The problem with the consumer culture is that it glorifies spending and vilifies frugality.

- Diligence as far as money is concerned is an exerted effort to learn all there is to know about money or to employ knowledge through use of professionals.

- Read every day, develop yourself and increase your knowledge and wisdom about your call and areas of interest.

- Grow in character; self-control, love, patience and kindness, understanding, knowledge and wisdom. Become wealthy inside before getting money.

# CHAPTER 6

# HOW THE RICH USE MONEY

*"Remember, young man, experience is not the best teacher. Other people's experience is the best teacher. By reading about the lives of great people, you can unlock the secrets to what made them great." Andy Andrews, Author Traveler's Gift: Seven Decisions that determine personal success.*

As we have seen from previous chapters, rich people do not behave like the masses. The world deceives people into believing that rich people are always the people driving the expensive cars, wearing luxury clothes and living in exclusive neighborhoods. You are made to think that to be rich all you have to be is to spend your money like the rich do. In the quests to be like the rich, people copy the lifestyle not knowing the secrets behind the lifestyles of the rich. People who are truly wealthy only spend money from the interest they make from their investments. They buy these luxury goods or plush lifestyle from their investments not their earnings. Wise people know the purpose of money. They understand the principles of money, how to spend money on what they need only so that they can invest money. Having money and also the lack of money is a result of the use of principles or the lack of use thereof.

This chapter shows you how the wise invest and the

135

sacrifices they make in order to make money work for them. It looks at these wise people from different income levels, from low income earner to high income earner and how they, through wisdom became rich. You, dear reader have to gain the understanding of the wise.

# HABITS OF THE RICH

### 1. The rich never work for money

Rich people never work for money; they let money work for them. Fear and greed motivate most people to work for money, for a salary. Fear of being without money and greed at all the *'things'* money can buy. The pattern of fear and greed; working harder out of fear of being without money and wanting more out of greed, keeps people trapped in the rat race. Rich people find a way out of that trap as fast as possible. They make uncomfortable sacrifices today to gain the future they want tomorrow. They are rich because they paid themselves and build their futures. The rich acquire assets while poor people acquire liabilities mistaking them for assets. The wealthy do not accumulate credit card debt buying liabilities. Credit cards usually have a window period within which no interest is charged as long as the debt is paid. If you do not have the discipline to use your card in this way, do not own a credit card. Not to belabor the point, the pitfalls of using credit cards and how to get out have been discussed in previous chapters.

### 2. The rich avoid spending their future.

Wealthy people invest money well through what they know and make it work for them. Wealthy people avoid spending their future. They pay themselves at least 20%

of their income. Wealthy people consider savings and investments two very different things and do not mix the two. Savings is not an investment and investments are not savings. Never lose money on savings. Money set aside as savings, as part of an emergency fund cannot be invested because you cannot afford to lose it. But setting aside such a fund prevents you from having to liquidate your investments in order to pay for emergencies. Imagine trying to sell a house during a housing slump to pay emergency bills. It's a guaranteed loss. The rich use emergency funds and insurance as tools to protect their gains. They do not just save, they take the next step and make wise investments. Contribute as much as possible towards investments. Have investments making at least 10% per annum and if possible over 30% per annum. The principle of compounding will then accelerate your wealth. That is how Warren Buffet made his money.

### 3. The rich mind their assets and only buy luxuries last.

The average annual return for Berkshire Hathaway, the company Warren Buffet controls, exceeds over 20% for over 40 years. Add to that the compounding factor and it's no wonder Warren Buffet has made himself and the shareholders in Berkshire Hathaway very wealthy. The rich mind their business, that is their assets and only buy luxuries last. Rich people have multiple sources of income. Because they have made wise investment choices they are able to multiply their money. It is from this investment income that they are able to fund their lifestyles. They do not rely on a salary; they focus on creating and building wealth. Middle class or poor people focus only on one or two sources of income. They depend on salary and focus on increasing their salary. When you pay yourself and focus on building a secure financial future you set yourself free and acquire the habits of the rich. In previous chapters, we saw how a man got to a crisis because he had not been saving any money and his children were about to go to college. Despite having a middle class income, he was spending all his money maintaining his lifestyle. My friend Raj is now making the same mistake, living an affluent life-style at the expense of savings and investments.

### 4. The rich do not gamble.

Poor people think wealth just happens. That is why poor people day dream and gamble a lot. Gambling is not a strategy to create wealth. You cannot sit idle and fantasize about how you will inherit money or what you will do when you win a million dollar jackpot. Unless you are doing it purely for entertainment and are ready to lose money, do not gamble. People who have built wealth do not gamble. They make investments in things that are certain to provide them with an investment return. They do not invest in hope stories or get rich quick schemes. They believe in creating the life they want. Find out through financial intelligence and the laws of money how to create wealth. If you follow these principles with diligence, persistence and focus, I guarantee you will be among the rich with time. These principles are practiced by the top billionaires and millionaires across the world. Money can be made using honest principles. The more than 200 millionaires that I have raised have proven that these principles work.

### 5. The rich read daily.

They think about ideas. They are constantly increasing

their knowledge of their areas of interest and investment. Studies have shown that 88% of the rich read for more than 30 minutes daily. 63% of them listen to audio books while commuting. 79% read educational career related materials. 55% read for personal development, 58% read biographies of successful people, 94% read current events and 51% read about history. Only 11% read purely for entertainment purposes[26]. Successful people read to improve themselves. Increasing in knowledge makes one able to spot opportunities resulting in money creation. In contrast only one in fifty people in financial difficulties improve themselves daily, most do not grow their skills and are easily retrenched after becoming obsolete. Wealthy people do not spend time watching TV or on the internet for leisure. Over 65% of them spend less than one hour on the internet for entertainment. Successful people manage their time well. They focus on personal development, networking, building businesses, volunteering or pursuits that will lead to more wealth. Of those with financial struggles, 77% spend more than an hour on TV, 74% more than an hour on the internet for entertainment. One of the first requirements we make of our members in the mentorship program that I run, is for them to study. We require them to study at least five books in a month. I spend at least 3 hours a day studying, I also advice the members to ensure they further their education. Those who come in with a Bachelor's Degree must pursue their Masters, and those with Masters Degrees should seek out their PHDs. We recognize these habits as important principles for life. We have testimonies of people who joined the church as students and as they studied became the best students in universities then social leaders and eventually ministers in government because they were diligent in studying.

### 6. The rich master their emotions.

Truly wealthy people are not ruled by their emotions, they do not let their emotions control them, especially when making financial decisions. Money does not dictate their mood. They have learnt how to act out of wisdom and not emotion. Wait, give yourself time to calm down and be objective before making decisions. Poor people are controlled a lot by fear; fear of failure, of change and other fears stop them from moving forward. Successful people learn to conquer their fear and build their confidence. Overcome the fear of failure by starting to invest money early and using the power of compounding in your favor. If you begin late you have to learn to take calculated risks and use financial intelligence to create money. Failure inspires winners. When confronted with failure, rich people do not run away from it, they seek answers.

### 7. The rich embrace change.

One of the members in a church was having repeated failure in the management of his finances. Each month he would find himself in debt, even when he would pray and fast, he would still find himself in debt the following month. Years went by and he continued to be in debt month after month. Finally he admitted his failure, he had tried to be financially successful but he was still in the vicious cycle of debt. He cried out to God and God led him to seek knowledge. He put aside all the money he had, that had actually been intended for bills and he went to a bookshop and bought every book he could find on debt and financial freedom. After studying the books and extracting the principles he began to apply them in his life. God put it in his heart to share the lessons he had learnt as a teacher and he set up seminars teaching on the topic of getting out of debt. Now he is financially free. He turned failure into victory. Poor people live in failure; they do not move on from failure but instead camp there. They allow fear or sorrow to prevent them from trying again. They wallow in pity parties and regret and build limiting beliefs around their failure. They believe the universe is against them, they were born unlucky and other negative beliefs. When people are afraid, they run away from change, they become rigid or do not move fast enough when change comes. The man who came out of debt was flexible to learn new things and change his habits and he became financially free. The only constant in life is change. Rich people embrace change. The wealthy invest in demolishing limiting believes and building beliefs that lead them to success. They credit their success to their beliefs. Poverty is a state of the mind, eliminate perspectives and beliefs that cause you to experience cycles of poverty, crisis and failure. People do not arrive at wealth by luck; even those who win lotteries do not keep the wealth unless they learn the laws of money. You have to be deliberate about becoming financially free.

### 8. The rich invest in building relationships.

Wealthy people invest in building relationships. They see the value in people. It is out of these networks that they receive ideas, market their products or get investment opportunities. Your environment determines your beliefs, motivates your actions. Build an environment of relationships around you that pushes you towards financial success.

# OVERCOME LIMITING BELIEFS

In the face of global poverty, many people have built beliefs about wealth and poverty. One common belief particularly in countries with high incidences of corruption is that you can only be rich through corrupt means. In Africa, some of the wealthiest men and women are wealthy as a result of corruption. The negative effect of corruption is that it makes people believe that their only way out of their poor situation or financial crisis is to take what is not theirs. Hence in such societies, theft, robberies and other crimes are prevalent. People believe that the system is rigged against them. Many of the wars and conflict in countries around Africa are as a result of such limiting beliefs. But there is an alternative to create wealth even for the poorest of the poor. The principles of wealth creation work for whoever applies them. If you have products that you offer, market and sell them, you make money. Looking at some of the poorest in African nations, you will notice they do not take time to differentiate their products or services. If a woman begins to sell vegetables in front of her house, within a week ten other women are selling the same vegetables outside their houses and the poor woman's business collapses. What if she took some little time to figure out her uniqueness and what she is passionate about? What if she can cook unique African dishes with her vegetables? Now instead of selling vegetables outside her house which every other woman is doing, she has unique recipes known only to her. She can then look for a market for her cooked food.

She can visit offices to sell packed lunches or supply cooked food to colleges. She can learn better ways to sell her products and increase the demand for her goods, and make more money. Such stories of people rising out of abject poverty exist, but they had to discover their uniqueness and pursue it. They were able to work hard at their businesses because they were passionate about the work, it wasn't a curse. God has given us everything that we need for life and godliness. He has given all of us, irrespective of poverty, the power to make wealth. Our purpose provides a key to unlocking the wealth in us. Know your purpose; the passion in it will drive you through hard times. Wealthy people are passionate about what they do. This makes them to go the extra mile. In an interview the late Steve Jobs had together with Bill Gates, he was asked how important passion was in building business. His response was classic, *'passion is what keeps you going when you encounter challenges in business.'* No wonder he was able to make a comeback at Apple even after losing his job in Apple years earlier.

## TRAPS OF THE RICH

Due to the money they have, rich people can also fall under the control of money. When they seek security and safety in their money they are trapped by the very money they seek safety in. That was the snare the rich young man found himself in[27]. He was unable to follow Jesus and find the satisfaction he was looking for because he could not do without his riches. At this point money was controlling him. When Jesus tried to deliver him from this prison, by advising him to sell all his riches and give to the poor, he went away sad but unable to do this. In fact Jesus admonishes after:

**"And again I say unto you, It is easier for a camel to go through the eye of a needle, than for a rich man to enter into the kingdom of God"**

*(Matthew 19:24)*

In this Bible verse, Jesus is not saying it is wrong to be rich but that for those who trust in riches they cannot be part of the Kingdom of God

When the story is retold in the gospel of Mark, Jesus is quoted as saying:

**"And the disciples were astonished at his words. But Jesus answered again, and said unto them, Children, how hard is it for them that trust in riches to enter into the kingdom of God!**

*(Mark 10:24)*

This does not mean that those who are wealthy cannot enter the Kingdom but they should not regard their wealth as above God. They should not trust in their riches. They should adopt the posture of Apostle Paul as though having nothing yet possessing everything. They should remain poor in spirit; that are still hungry for God and the things He has to offer so that they can have the Kingdom of God. To be poor in spirit is to keep a humble heart, ready to learn and ready to receive from God. Sometimes men and women who experience great financial abundance become proud and before God cannot receive anything.

**"Blessed are the poor in spirit: for theirs is the kingdom of heaven"**

*(Matthew 5:3)*

**Money is a good tool and provides answers to various problems.**

It is easy to move attention away from God and depend on the solutions money can provide. The rich begin to trust in their riches and not anymore on God. The Bible teaches that those who do this pierce themselves with many sorrows. There are countless stories of people who derived their identities from money and once they lost all their money, they could not continue with their lives and committed suicide. There are others yet who were not rich but they dedicated all their energies and time to become rich with the hope that money would satisfy them. Many of these people were disappointed. Rich people will testify that money only provides happiness up to a certain point, where your needs are satisfied. Once your needs are satisfied any extra money does not bring about any additional satisfaction. A number of the world's richest people as per Forbes magazine annual wealth ranking are giving away most of their wealth or pledging to give it away during their lifetimes. If having all the money was so satisfying why would these billion-aires choose to give it away?

Corruption is a cancer in countries around the world. Greed and the love of money drive the people who enrich themselves through corruption. Some of the poorest countries in the world have the richest leaders in the world courtesy of corruption. Wealthy people are not those who steal from their nations to enrich themselves.

These people are controlled by money. That is not our definition of wealth.

**People who take money that is intended for the collective good of others and use it for their own gain are evil and their end is nothing.**

The example of the life of Mobutu Sese Seko is one illustration. Reported at one point to be worth billions of dollars while his country was one of the poorest in the world, he died a miserable death, disgraced and exiled from Zaire. We have seen particularly in developing countries money intended to provide vaccines for poor children being siphoned by government officials or nonprofit organizations to enrich themselves. Such riches attract a curse and are of no benefit to society. Wealth is meant to bring solutions and the betterment of society. Money does not satisfy when used outside the cause of advancing the Kingdom of God and His right order. It only corrupts, controls and ruins lives.

On the other hand masses of the poor only followed Jesus because He had fed them. The only value they could see in Him was food. The thinking behind the poverty mindset is only in having their needs met, therefore they sell their time, their most valuable commodity for salary, a token just enough to meet their expenses. The story of Esau is true every day; people sell off their birthright (their future inheritance) for today's food. Surrender your material possessions to God to escape the trap of money. Learn to place value on what God places value on, for where your treasure is there your heart is. Abraham kept his focus on God not on his riches. In Hebrews 11:9-11, he would not be satisfied in what he had but kept looking for the city that God was building. When you dominate money, God can now trust you with true riches. True riches are where God opens Himself to you and invites you to rule with Him.

In looking at the culture of the rich there are important lessons to be learnt. As you have gone through this chapter you realize that what makes someone rich is not their lifestyle but their mindset, their perspective on life. The rich also learn to control themselves. In the next chapter we would look at controlling yourself and the appetites of your ego. This is an important element we have seen in the lives of the wealthy and which we would look at in more detail next. It is important to keep in mind the following nuggets from this chapter.

## WISDOM TO APPLY

1. Identify the top 10 persons in your area of passion both in your country and internationally and find out all you can about them. Extract life principles from their lives and apply them. Learn from their failures also.

2. Living like the rich is not by copying their life-styles but by mimicking their habits. Look at how the rich manage their money and invest their time and learn those habits. Don't buy what they buy or wear what they wear rather invest more in knowing what they know.

3. Learn to trust God and do not to put your trust in riches. You may not be rich, you may be experiencing poverty or financial crisis, but you can still fall into the trap of trusting in riches. Develop trust in God through His word and fellowship with Him.

# GOLDEN NUGGETS

- Credit cards usually have a window period within which no interest is charged as long as the debt is paid. If you do not have the discipline to use your card in this way, do not own a credit card.

- The rich use emergency funds and insurance as tools to protect their gains.

- Middle class or poor people focus only on one or two sources of income.

- The rich do not invest in hope stories or get rich quick schemes.

- Only one in fifty people in financial difficulties improve themselves daily, most do not grow their skills and are easily retrenched after becoming obsolete.

- Overcome the fear of failure by starting to invest money early and using the power of compounding in your favor.

- The wealthy invest in demolishing limiting beliefs and building beliefs that lead them to success.

- Build an environment of relationships around you that pushes you towards financial success.

- Our purpose provides a key to unlocking the wealth in us. Know your purpose; the passion in it will drive you through hard times.

- Wealth is meant to bring solutions and the betterment of society.

# CHAPTER 7
# CONTROL YOUR APPETITE

*"The enemy of God, Satan, came in to take advantage of human needs (for food, protection and pleasure) to organize a system in order to systematize people." Basic Principles of the Experience of Life by Witness Lee*

In a previous chapter we saw that the world system takes advantage of your legitimate human needs to control you. The quotation above from Witness Lee, one of the Christian leaders of the spread of Christianity in China in the early 1900s, shows this tactic of Satan. Satan uses basic human needs and corrupts human desire into lust. For example, you need to wear clothes; it's a basic human need. You see an advertisement for luxury clothes telling you to *"reward yourself, successful people only wear the very best"*, which happens to be the brand they are advertising. You are then enticed to spend thousands of dollars on clothing yet you can get good clothes for just hundreds of dollars. To be able to outsmart this push, you have to put your desires in check, to control your ego so to speak. Once you understand who you are and what you are trying to achieve, you can forego some comforts and reduce your expenses to increase your savings.

# CHECK YOURSELF

The Bible[28] teaches that all that is in the world that is the lust of the flesh, the lust of the eyes and the pride of life are not from God but from the world. Herein is the trick the world system uses. Whatever is inside you is what is used to control you!

**But every man is tempted, when he is drawn away of his own lust, and enticed. Then when lust has conceived, it brings forth sin: and sin, when it is finished, brings forth death.**
*(James 1:14-15)*

We are advised not to love the world. The *'world'* here signifies the system of rule and the perspective and way of thinking that is in place in the world. All it comprises of is pride and lust.

What are these three things that are said to be of the world? The lust of the flesh, the lust of the eyes and the pride of life. Lust is actually a perverted desire. It is not limited only to perverse sexual desire. Your own legitimate desires become corrupted and are turned into depravities. When you seek satisfaction in things for what only God can satisfy, then this persuasion happens.

## THE LUST OF THE FLESH

The lust of the flesh refers to that which pampers your desires, indulgences that sooth the corrupted part of your body or soul; that is the flesh. A person concerned with doing only that which pleases their body and titillates their minds is driven by the lust of the flesh. Obesity is a growing problem in the populations of some developed countries. Part of what drives it is the desire to keep experiencing pleasure from food. So much so that even when one is not hungry they still eat because they are seeking the satisfaction from eating, the pleasure that comes from eating good food. A lot of women around the world confess to eating foods not because they are hungry but for comfort. They are seeking the pleasure from the food to comfort them. They may be stressed out, depressed, sad, grieving or discontent with life and so they eat to try to find that satisfaction in food. The same happens mostly to women when it comes to shopping. The thrill of buying whether clothes or shoes or bags excites the body and the emotions providing a 'high'. Shopaholics will confess chasing this high over and over again until they become addicted to shopping. A person may be seeking satisfaction out of deep emptiness or deep hunger, which in itself is not the problem. The problem comes when one tries to find satisfaction in food or in shopping for a spiritual hunger.

You cannot satisfy spiritual hunger with material things, spiritual hunger can only be satisfied by God. That is what the Samaritan woman discovered. She had been trying to satisfy her hunger through men and even though she had had five husbands and the one she was living with wasn't her husband she wasn't still satisfied. It was only when she encountered Jesus that she found what she hungered for. In the same way seeking to satisfy these hungers by gratifying the demands of our bodies or our minds only leads to addiction. The number of addictions even to everyday things in the world is high. Addictions to food, to sleeping, to drinking, to drugs, to shopping, to sex, to touch are rampant. Even when we are not driven by addictions a lot of times we are driven by this lust. When buying shoes for example, you might be driven not by the need to protect your feet but by the thrill of buying new shoes. There is a thrill that comes with having something new. The advertising and product marketing feeds into this because they understand this is a more powerful drive that is stronger than even the need. You are constantly being prodded to please yourself. Treat yourself well, feel the high, delight yourself, pursue the thrill, reward yourself and so on. Success is marketed to us as being able to get whatever we could possibly want!

## THE LUST OF THE EYES

The lust of the eyes refers to the desire to gratify the sight. The luxury clothes, the sparkling jewels, the beautiful handcrafted furniture, private jets and exotic vacation spots, these appeal to your eyes. Eve, tempted by Satan, saw that the fruit he was giving her was good for food and was pleasant to the eyes, and so she ate it and man fell into sin. Satan appealed to her using her eyes. Because of the fallen nature in you, your body and your mind seek things that please the sight, things that have no eternal value, frivolities and vanities of the world. It doesn't mean that we should not appreciate beautiful things and even want them; we should not be driven by what we see but by the Spirit of God. When we are driven by what we see, we end up seeking the things we see to satisfy us, hoping material things satisfy where only God can satisfy.

Have you noticed that adverts that sell even the most basic things like bathing soap, have a picture of a 'beautiful' woman? What does a woman have to do with soap? Advertisers are enticing you with your own eyes; they know you will associate the soap with either having the beautiful woman or being like the beautiful woman. You will notice as you shop in the supermarket that certain things are put in the front where you queue up to pay for your shopping. Chocolate, candy, mints things that appeal to your eyes are put there to tempt you into impulse buying.

## THE PRIDE OF LIFE

The pride of life is also of the world. Pride refers to an unreasonable conceit of one's own superiority in talents, beauty, wealth, accomplishments, rank or elevation in office. It manifests itself in lofty airs, distance, reserve, and often in contempt of others[29]. It is often described in such terms as to pride one's self, to indulge pride; to take pride; to value one's self; to gratify self-esteem. The world values achievement, accomplishments and status. People pride themselves in their wealth, dress or status. They pride themselves in their achievements. Yet we all want to be applauded, to be accepted and to be valued highly. Even poor people are constantly seeking identity and status. The pride of life is the corruption of these desires. Where we seek to be applauded, to be accepted and to be valued by men far much more than we seek to be applauded, accepted and valued highly by God, the pride of life flourishes. When we value the esteem of men much higher than the esteem of God, we will then do whatever it takes to gain attention from people, to please and be accepted by people. The societal pressure and peer pressure will constantly drive us. We will live in areas that have a certain status, drive cars that are admired by people and spend money on things that give us status and admiration. Even when we do not have the money to buy these things we will drive ourselves hard, working to acquire the money for such things. We will not be able to do what God wants because we are conscious of men and what they think of us.

Unless we are delivered from these three problems, we will keep struggling with how we spend money. We may have good intentions and will embrace the teachings in this book with gladness and joy, but these things will pull us back even when we begin to implement the taught principles. These lusts will drive you and combined with the love of money, you will spend your life seeking to satisfy these lusts and the pursuit of money. We must uproot these corrupted desires in us first. That is what Paul taught, that we should no longer be as the world is but should be changed by a complete 180 degrees turn of our thinking to mirror how God thinks and then we could do as God wants[30]. We can be freed in our minds to pursue the will of God for our lives. Again, it all starts with re-educating our minds and being led by the Holy Spirit. If I teach you how to be financially successful but not how to avoid being controlled by money; you will not fulfill the purpose of God and live for God. Money will ruin you. It is important to deal with yourself so that you are no longer controlled by lusts and pride; the tools the world system uses.

# AS JESUS CHRIST WAS ON THE EARTH SO ARE WE

Look at how Jesus dealt with these things. The Holy Spirit led Jesus before the beginning of His public ministry to a desert to be tempted[31]. Jesus was tempted in these three areas; the lust of the flesh, the pride of life and the lust of the eyes. He was tempted to meet his need for food first, to satisfy his flesh; the lust of the flesh. He had a legitimate desire for food. He had not eaten anything in weeks! His response was, you are not to live to satisfy your body alone, but for something higher, you are to fulfill the commands of God and the direction of God. To overcome the lust of the flesh, you must be driven by the Spirit of God. You must live for the Kingdom of God and His agenda. All your energies and your money must be directed towards His Kingdom. If you are seeking to set yourself free from the world system, it is so that you can use your time to advance the Kingdom of God in your sphere of influence.

**"This I say then, Walk in the Spirit, and you shall not fulfill the lust of the flesh"**
*(Galatians 5:16)*

His desire was to do the will of God more than it was for any pleasure the world could give Him.
In John 4:34 Jesus said unto them:

**"My meat is to do the will of him that sent me, and to finish his work".**

The second temptation for Jesus was to satisfy the pride of life. The temptation was for him to show and

157

display that indeed He was the son of God. If indeed He was the Son of God, the devil pushed Him to prove it. God does not need to prove who He is; He already knows who He is. The world offers us the same temptation. When you have a good salary, you need to show that indeed you are the manager of that company or the CEO of a big company, by living in a certain neighborhood or driving a particular brand of car or joining an exclusive club. You need to know who you are, what God has made you to be and you will not need to prove yourself to men. You will not seek affirmation from men. The more you know God, the more He reveals to you who you are and the less you need to prove anything to men.

The final temptation was to give in to the lust of the eyes. Satan showed Jesus what he could give him, the splendor and the glory of kingdoms. All He had to do was value that splendor and the glory of these things above God. We too face the same temptation, money can provide a glorious lifestyle, and we can have beautiful cars that our incomes can buy. But we must resist pursuing those things as our primary goal. If we do not, we cannot deny ourselves today so that we can build the future we want. We must not have those attractive things now. When we seek first the kingdom of God and His righteousness all these other things will be added too[32]. Jesus sought God's Kingdom first, He valued God more highly and God exalted Him above all those kingdoms and gave Him a name above every other name.

## WISDOM FOR SELF-CONTROL

Involve God in your plans. Most Christians somehow believe that once they have given their tithes and offerings, God has no more say in what they do with the rest of the money. When you make Jesus Christ your Lord, you agree to have Him direct your entire life, including your finances. As you come up with your budget, your shopping lists, let God direct you so that you can learn to be led by the Spirit of God and not your desires. These lusts and pride of life, war with our spirits and the Spirit of God and it is only through renewing your mind and obeying the leading of God that you begin to overcome them. This means that we no longer live according to the lusts, but according to the will of God. We become driven not by wanting to have money and the things that money affords us but to live for the calling and purpose of God for our lives.

## BUILD A PRISON
## AROUND YOUR LIFE

Build a prison around your life that makes it easier to live according to your calling and not according to the dictates of money. Ladies, if you find yourselves struggling constantly with buying clothes, shoes and bags that you do not need, avoid going into shopping malls and places that provide such temptations. Find activities in line with your calling that take away your attention and need for such things. If you are a cook, volunteer some of your time to teach others the basics of cooking, for example. Plan your activities so that you do not have idle time, develop yourself in your calling and spend more time with God in prayer and in His word to strengthen yourself.

Control your ego; begin by refusing to care about what others think of you. If you find yourself tempted to buy things so as to impress others, stop. Overcome your own desire to be honored or applauded. Live as though you do not have the things you have. Don't drive around the neighborhood so that everyone can see your new car. Leave your car at home sometimes, and take public transport, it shows your identity is not in the car. Stop caring about what others think of you. 75% of people only think about themselves, they do not care to think about you. The famous designer Coco Chanel was quoted once as saying *"I don't care what you think about me, I don't think about you at all."*

If you don't adopt this attitude then it will be difficult for you to downgrade your life for fear of what people will think of you. Let them think you are broke because you sold your car, or because you moved your children out of the exclusive private school, it's only you who knows what you are doing and it's you and your family that will benefit in the future. Don't build your life based on people's opinions. If you are trying to impress people, it's easy for them to take advantage of you. You end up lending money to people, because you want them to like you and at the end they don't pay you back. They will still end up hating you or envying you for whatever reason even if you spend all your money on them. Focus on impressing God!

Control your desires especially when it comes to buying things for your children. Ensure your children learn to value you for you, not what they can get from you. Teach your children to value the intangibles; love, companionship, fellowship, kindness, relationships and the like.

Do not be too quick to spend money. Take time as you

budget to evaluate why you want what you are buying. Make it hard for yourself to spend money quickly. You can limit how much money you carry or eliminate carrying money at all. I have formed a habit of not carrying any money with me. You may want to carry only what you have budgeted to spend on that day for essentials, such as transportation. Also avoid carrying debit cards and credit cards that provide you easy access to money. In the end you have to learn to deny yourself, be sober about your reasons for wanting the things you desire and only buy what you need. Train yourself to live this way, not only as a way to reduce your spending but as a way to deny these lustful desires and pride.

## MONEY DOES NOT DETERMINE YOUR WORTH

It is not money that should determine your value, your status, your worth, your emotions and your desires. You are who God says you are. You are not inferior to someone else because you are poor neither are you better than everybody else just because you have money. God made you in His image and likeness. He has put himself in you and desires to express who He is through you, through your gifts and talents. To him who is poor, watch out that you are not trying to be rich to become somebody. To him who is rich, watch out that your possessions do not possess you. Make sure you can live without them and are not living in fear of losing it all. Jesus' philosophy was that one should behave as though he doesn't have. How do you do this? Think, if you didn't have your material possessions, without your spouse, without your children, would you still be content?

Let's look at some of the people's lives in previous examples. Raj is quite content with his comfortable lifestyle. If we examine his motives we might be able to see that perhaps the reason he is unwilling to change his lifestyle to acquire more investments is because money defines him. His current life presents him in a good image to his peers and he is not willing to lose that. The teacher whose wife was selling snacks at his workplace had to endure ridicule from his colleagues who thought his wife is doing a menial job not fit for the wife of a teacher. But he chooses to ignore his colleagues. Martin on the other hand accumulated $50,000 in consumer debt buying things he couldn't afford because he wanted them. He bought new furniture for his house because he felt it was a need at the time. Now after looking back he realizes he should only have bought such things after investing his money and generating income from it. Even though his home may need some upgrades now, he can wait until his investments provide him an income before making such purchases. Sometimes though like Thomas or Julia one does not realize that the decisions they make unconsciously lead them to the financial crisis they find themselves in. Having a high consumer lifestyle out of pressure from society without much conscious thought is what led them to the situations they found themselves. It had to take unpleasant situations for them to wake up from such passivity and take action to build their futures. Does it have to take sickness or financial crisis to wake you up to take action to build a secured financial future? No it does not. Please do not wait for such tragic situations to happen before you could start to pay yourself. In the next chapter we look at how you can build your future by bringing to reality the dreams in your heart.

# SELF CONTROL ACTION PLAN

1. Spend time with God and His word daily to renew your mind, change your thinking to be conformed to His. If we are truly rich in God, we will not be using houses and cars to define ourselves.

2. Take time before spending money to determine your motive for buying what you want to buy. Examine your inner thoughts regularly. You will be surprised how much lust and pride is the motive behind your expenditure.

3. Limit your access to money and plan your spending so that you avoid impulse buying.

4. Deny yourself. Do not buy everything that pleases you. Buy only what you need.

5. Control your ego. Embrace humility. Change your lifestyle to reduce your spending even when it hurts your public image. The desire to live big to impress people already puts you in captivity of money.

# GOLDEN NUGGETS

- A person may be seeking satisfaction out of deep emptiness or deep hunger, which in itself is not the problem. The problem comes when one tries to find satisfaction in food or in shopping for a spiritual hunger.

- Success is marketed to us as being able to get whatever we could possibly want!

- Because of the fallen nature in you, your body and your mind seek things that please the sight, things that have no eternal value, frivolities and vanities of the world.

- The pride of life is the corruption of these desires.

- If you are seeking to set yourself free from the world system, it is so that you can use your time to advance the Kingdom of God in your sphere of influence.

- You need to know who you are, what God has made you to be and you will not need to prove yourself to men. You will not seek affirmation from men.

- The lusts and pride of life, war with our spirits and the Spirit of God and it is only through renewing your mind and obeying the leading of God that you could overcome them.

- You end up lending money to people because you want them to like you and they end up not paying you back.

- Avoid carrying debit cards and credit cards that provide you easy access to money.

- To him who is poor, watch out that you are not trying to be rich to become somebody. To him who is rich, watch out that your possessions do not possess you.

# CHAPTER 8
# BUILD YOUR FUTURE

*'The future belongs to those who believe in the beauty of their dreams.' Eleanor Roosevelt. Eleanor Roosevelt is a former first lady of the United States. She was married to the American president Franklin Roosevelt who was president during the 1920s and 1930s, during a period of great financial difficulties. She lays an important point. Your future lies in your dreams. You have to discover how to make these dreams a reality. Have you uncovered your dreams? Are you pursuing them?*

In 1995 Jack Ma, a former English teacher, visited the United States for the first time. Out of that visit, he discovered the internet and realized that his country, *China*, was not well represented on the internet. When he searched the word China in the computer the search came up with no information on China. He realized through the internet, a lot of companies from his home could sell their products all over the world. From that point on Jack Ma dedicated his time to achieving that goal despite failures and setbacks. The first company he founded failed and he had to take up a job with the Chinese government. He eventually founded Alibaba in 1999. He raised $60,000 from 17 of his friends and colleagues and set out to build a company that could compete with any other company in the world, including the market leaders in the United States. For three years the company did not make any revenues, instead funding its expenses from investor money raised. A series of mistakes almost threw them out of business, at one point they were spending $2 million dollars a month and only had $10 million in their accounts giving them only 5 months to survive. Jack and his team restructured the business increasing membership on the online platform and turning a profit of $10 million. Once they found a way to make money, the company continued to expand and grow despite challenges and competition from EBay in China. In September 2014 Alibaba sold some of its shares to the public through an Initial Public Offering (IPO) in the New York Securities Exchange; NYSE as the largest ever listing of any company. In fact it was the largest IPO in the world history raising $21.8 billion. Alibaba was valued at over $100 billion dollars and Jack Ma's personal fortune had jumped to almost $20 billion dollars. He had moved from being an English teacher in the early 1990s earning less than 200$ a month to one of the wealthiest men in the world![34]

## HOW TO START BUILDING YOUR FUTURE

By now dear reader, from our previous chapters I hope you realize that the ultimate objective of securing your financial future is to be able to focus on building your future life. We all have greatness in us. The difference between those who unlock it and those who don't is time. If you spend all your time to fulfill your basic needs and vanities of this world, you will never unlock your greatness. Once you are free from the bondage of salary, organize all your time towards discovery and fulfillment of your purpose here on earth. Your purpose should advance the kingdom of God and His righteousness in a particular area. Malcolm Gladwell in his book, *Outliers*, discusses case studies of great and respected men in our day. He proposes what is now known as the 10,000-Hour Rule. The rule states that 10,000 hours of deliberate practice are needed to achieve mastery in any field. Examples of the lives of men with such great accomplishments such as Bill Gates, golfer Tiger Woods and celebrated musicians such as the Beatles show that they invested a lot of time working on their craft from an early age before they became experts. For you to become great in your area of call, you will need to invest time. If all your time is taken up by a job that is not leading you towards your call, how will you ever unlock your greatness? You must learn to pay yourself and build a secured financial future so that you can free up your time to actualize your greatness.

## AVERAGE PEOPLE, EXTRAOR-DINARY RESULTS

All throughout the book we have looked at why we need to pay ourselves. We have looked at setting up financial plans that are in line with your calling to enable you to work for your calling not for money. How then do you build your future? Let's look at some examples.

Helena joined God's Embassy Church eighteen years ago. She was 17 years old and freshly out of school. The situation in the country at the time was quite difficult. The Soviet Union had collapsed and the economy was bad. Soviet culture at the time, taught communism, that everyone should be the same. People were very passive about their lives. She took some of the lessons I was teaching in church and determined to be the best student at her university. She studied hard and made sacrifices to study while her classmates were out having fun. She knew in her mind she was doing all this to promote the Kingdom of God. After her undergraduate study, she proceeded to do her masters and was voted the best post-graduate student. This opened up opportunities as civil society leader. When she went back to do her PHD in science, she got an opportunity to work with some of the best minds in her country in science and innovation. She dedicated herself to building her dream and today she is a scientist influencing her field for God.

Do you know what happened to the teacher's wife in the previous example I had given?. As the teacher realized that his wife could multiply their savings, he kept investing in her business and she kept growing it until eventually over two years she set up her own restaurant employing 20 people and generating income of over $5,000 a month in a country where the average income is below $300. The teacher was able to quit his job and together with his wife, they are now working towards setting up franchises across their city.

Strive Masiyiwa is the founder, chairman and CEO of Econet Wireless Holdings, an international telecommunications group based in South Africa with operations in three continents. Born in 1961 into the British Colony of Rhodesia, now Zimbabwe, his family fled the country to settle into the neighboring Zambia, when the colonial government began to fall apart. His mother was an entrepreneur and his father a mine worker who later joined the family business. Masiyiwa grew up learning entrepreneurship from an early age by observing his parents.

By age 12, his parents sent him to school in Scotland. He went on to earn a degree in Electrical and Electronic Engineering from the University of Wales. Once back in Zimbabwe, he worked with the government rising to the position of principal engineer but left when he became frustrated with the government bureaucracy to start his own business in electrical contracting.

*"It took me about five years to build my first business. It was not unusual for me to spend 48 hours at the business non-stop."*[35]

In the early 1990s he recognized a potential business opportunity. Sub-Saharan Africa had 2 landline telephones for every 100 people at the time. He had a solution to this problem, mobile phones. He sold his company and decided to pursue this opportunity. Despite great opposition he succeeded in starting a cell phone network in Botswana and eventually in Zimbabwe. His company, Econet Wireless Holdings valued at over $750 Million, went on to set up in over 15 countries including other African countries, the United Kingdom and New Zealand. Masiyiwa has expanded to other businesses and uses his platform to advance education and economic development across Africa. He attributes his success partly to the study and practice of his craft. Once in an interview with CNN[i] he was asked,

*"Do you read the Bible for an hour every day? Is that correct? I've read that."*

Masiyiwa's response was:

---

i     Cable News Network, broadcasting out of the United States

*"Oh, that's when I'm busy. I can read it for four or five hours on the weekend."*

He once spent two years studying banking in order to ask for a small business loan. He learnt the language of the golf course and of the balance sheet because,

*"In the money game, there is a way of talking that will have bankers and investors interested in what you want to do, and there is a way to talk which makes them shun and run away from you, and it has nothing to do with where you come from."*[36]

## FREE YOUR TIME TO UNLOCK GREATNESS

If you pay yourself, you set yourself free from the world system and you can now start investing in your future. This will enable you to dedicate your time to unlocking your own greatness as your money works for you. Being frugal does not mean that you will not have the standard of life that you desire. It does not mean that you will not own luxurious homes, yachts or jets if you so desire. It means you plan out these things into your future as the Spirit of God leads you. Since you have deferred comfort to the future, you can build yourself as your investments work for you. You have an opportunity to succeed in wealth creation, by building the future you see, and then you can have access to these things.

Napoleon Hill, in his famous book, *Think and Grow Rich*, tells the story of a man by the name Edwin Barnes. Edwin Barnes had a burning desire to become a business associate of Thomas Edison, but he was poor and disadvantaged. He set about finding a way to go to the state where Edison was located to meet with him. When he met him, he introduced himself and stated his desire to become Thomas Edison's' partner. Even though he was not impressive physically, Edison gave Edwin Barnes the chance to work for him. Months went by and Barnes continued to work for Edison, not in a business partnership, working for Edison. But in those months, Barnes continued to build himself in the desire to become Edison's partner. Eventually an opportunity came to sell one of Edison's machines and Barnes so excelled at selling this machine that Edison made him a business partner. Edwin Barnes eventually became rich from this partnership.

Scientist, George Washington Carver is renowned for having over a hundred different inventions. He is the father of over 100 uses for the peanut. One time, George Washington Carver spent over 5 days straight on his work locked up in his office, not eating, just taking drinks, while working on his invention. All his workers got worried about him and by the fifth day, they broke down his door. Startled, he turned around and asked them what the problem was. He said, he had just come in that same morning and was doing his work. The workers informed a surprised Carver that he had been in his office for five days! That is why he was one of the greatest inventors in history. He combined his passion, focus, energy and time and dedicated it to his calling.

# BECOME GREAT

What do all these people have in common? They dedicated their time and energy to achieving their visions. If you are going to fulfill your purpose and become great in your area of calling, you will have to dedicate your time and energy to achieve these things. You can use time to become anything in your heart to become. You are not going to become great trapped in the world system earning a salary, doing a job you do not enjoy. Paying yourself is your ticket out! And once you have freed yourself, you must dedicate your time persistently towards spending every second, every minute to fulfilling your calling. If your time currently is mortgaged for a salary, you only have very little time within a day towards working on yourself. Your employer certainly will not pay you to do things that are not adding to his bottom line, he owns your time.

If you consistently discipline yourself to paying yourself every month and then you multiply this money, you should be able to be free from depending on a salary in 3 to 5 years. Then from that point on you can dedicate your time fully without interruptions to building your God-given dreams. Because your money is working for you, you will have the focus like Strive Masiyiwa, George Washington Carver and Jack Ma to persevere difficulties, failures and other challenges to bring these dreams into a reality.

You can unlock great wealth when you dedicate your time in your area of passion and calling. The principles of wealth creation work best when you focus on the areas you are passionate about because it is not a burden to spend time researching and coming up with goods and services to offer the world. You find joy and fulfillment in doing what you are passionate about. That is why you need to be free. Your hope for your future is in your passions, in your calling. When you work in your area of calling you are as effective as a laser beam of light. Because of the concentrated energy, the results you get are far much greater than you get doing just any work. Your productivity in an hour goes up and this has a direct impact on your net worth.

Natalie, another member of our network of churches in Ukraine, joined the church in her early twenties. She had gotten married at age 18. Her husband was a businessman and she focused on helping him and raising her young family. When the husband became successful in business he became unfaithful to her and eventually left her. At her lowest, she did not see the value of life and she had to be supported to feed her children by the church. After going through my trainings, she began to discover herself, her own self-worth and her purpose. Her purpose was connected with women and out of her own experience she began to help women through women clubs to discover themselves and their inherent worth and calling. She turned this into a business conducting training for women and she saw her business grow. She invested in developing herself, studying 4 to 5 books a month and being part of my trainings some lasting as long as 18 hours a day. From what she learnt, she went out and partnered with a fellow church member and started to offer business coaching to entrepreneurs. They would hold seminars and business lunches to train businessmen and women on how to start businesses and how to be competitive in the business world. She was also using both the women clubs and business lunches to introduce the Kingdom of God to her clients. She began to mentor and disciple them through online platforms. Together with her business partner, they would pray for the entrepreneurs over their problems, lead many to salvation, teach them to pray, and lead them to baptism of the Holy Spirit. Her business has grown and still she is constantly thinking of how to use the business to spread the Kingdom of God. She has realized no matter how much money people have they are still in need of Christ. Because of her own success, she is bold to take the gospel of the kingdom to wealthy businessmen in her city.

## EXCELLENCE, A KEY TO GREATNESS

The higher the quality of goods and services you produce, the more you are rewarded for your labor. Unfortunately many people in the world spend so much time hating what they do that they become mediocre at their work. Monday morning is the worst day of the week for a lot of people. They wake up to go to jobs they do not enjoy and many suffer from the *Monday blues*. On the other hand, Friday is the day they are most thankful to God for. They are glad they are going into the weekend and do not have to work. With such an attitude you can never produce quality results. You can never truly excel until you produce high quality work. Yet for us as Christians work is how we create just like God did. In Isaiah 65:22, God promises that his elect shall long enjoy the work of their hands. Once you have discovered your call and have freed yourself from the world system, use your passion to ensure you produce quality work. This is your secret to rising. When you become better than everyone else at what you do then you can command great influence and money. Men will come from far to search for you.

In 1949, a young man by the name Frank McCourt arrived in the United States of America in search of the American dream. He had been raised in the slums of Roden Street in Limerick in Ireland, where his mother did odd jobs to make ends meet. His father had abandoned the family when he was 13 years old. He had worked at different menial jobs and saved part of his income for his big dream, to go to America. When in the United States, he served in the United States Army during the Korean War. When he was discharged from the army, he used his privilege as a veteran to enroll in a university completing his Bachelors and then a Master's degree in 1967. While in school, he still had to take up odd jobs to support himself. After his studies, he secured a job as a public school teacher, teaching English and eventually creative writing in various schools. He taught for over a period of 30 years, during which time he discovered his calling as a writer. Upon his retirement and on the urging of his family, he wrote his memoir titled, *Angela's Ashes* in 1996. The book was a commercial success selling over 5 million copies worldwide, published in 27 countries and translated into 17 languages. The book turned him into a millionaire almost overnight. Frank McCourt became famous and gained critical acclaim. He received various awards, the National Book Critics Circle award in 1996 and one of the highest awards for a writer, the Pulitzer Prize in 1997, on his very first novel. He had spent over

30 years of his life discovering his calling as a writer and learning to write that book.[37]

## LIVE FOR YOUR PURPOSE

Less than 20% of people living in the world today are living for their purpose. Many are spending their lives depressed, trapped and unable to do what is in their heart. The tragedy of the world is that the vast majority of its people are not pursuing their calling. They are living to survive, eking out a living day by day. People concerned with only their stomachs can only produce mediocre products. The dreams and hopes of generations lie dead in graveyards across the continents of the world. Much more in Africa, Is it any wonder why Africa is the poorest continent in the world? If you succeed in setting yourself free from the world system, you are better than 80% of the world. If you go a step further and utilize your time to build your future, you will change your life and the lives of countless others for generations to come. Become part of the minority and step into your uniqueness.

I will give you another example, this time of a young girl aged 21, a member in one of our churches. At 17 she was living with her boyfriend and they had a child together. As they continued living together Anastasia realized that her boyfriend was a drug addict. In an effort to help him, she searched her city for a rehabilitation centre and the only place she could find help was the church and its drug rehabilitation program. She only committed to be a member of the church so that her boyfriend could receive help to overcome the addiction, but as she continued to attend, she started learning the principles of life. She realized she had a purpose and a unique call and that her worth was not determined by her relationships. She made the decision to start supporting herself and get out of her sinful relationship. At 18, she set up beauty centers where she would provide personal beauty services and teach women to look after their bodies. She would also conduct trainings where she taught women, young and old, how to discover themselves and their value. From her business she is able to pay herself and still support her child. As she continued with her business, she discovered her calling in the media; she wanted to become a television newscaster. She used part of her savings and enrolled in the university to study journalism and she is currently pursuing a Masters' degree in journalism and media. She had grown up in a culture that teaches that the destiny of a woman was marriage and children and that she could only be supported by men. That is how she had ended up living with someone and pregnant. She was able to change her beliefs, overcome laziness and build a business through diligence, save and invest. She is building her own future and her son's future.

As we conclude this chapter, I have summarized below steps to build your future. Spend some time reading and thinking over them, then implement the answers unique to your life. Once you have the answers to the questions, then you can move on to the next chapter. In the following chapter, we would look at what to do with the money you have saved and how to make that money work for you, the options for general investment available.

# CONCRETE STEPS TO BUILD YOUR FUTURE

1. Find your area of calling.
2. What will you do once you have gotten back your time that will make you better?
3. How can you use the knowledge you gain to help you fulfill your call?
4. Convert every minute of the day into adding value in your area of calling. Research deeply, study and acquire as much knowledge in your area of calling as there is. Focus your time on your area of calling to research and to build products and services to offer to the world.
5. Ensure you produce good quality goods and services and keep improving on the quality of your products. Whatever your hands find to do, do it with all your heart.
6. Learn how to create demand for your good or service. As you come up with quality goods and services, ensure that they will meet needs in society, then dedicate time to learning how to create demand for them.

# GOLDEN NUGGETS

- You must learn to pay yourself and build a secured financial future so that you can free up your time to actualize your greatness.

- Being frugal does not mean that you will not have the standard of life that you desire.

- Paying yourself is your ticket out! And once you have freed yourself, you must dedicate your time persistently towards spending every second, every minute to fulfilling your calling.

- When you work in your area of calling you are as effective as a laser beam of light. Because of the concentrated energy, the results you get are far much greater than you get doing just any work.

- The higher the quality of goods and services you produce, the more you are rewarded for your labor.

- If you succeed in setting yourself free from the world system, you are better than 80% of the world. Become part of the minority and step into your uniqueness.

# CHAPTER 9

# INVESTMENTS

*"Investing is most intelligent when it is most businesslike." Benjamin Graham, Author of the Intelligent Investor. Benjamin Graham is said to be the father of value investing, a strategy of investment that one of the richest men in the world, Warren Buffet follows. It seeks to find investment opportunities that are below their actual value and to profit from these investment opportunities when they eventually come into their true worth.*

When he was 25 years old in 1956, Warren Buffett started a partnership focused on investing, Buffet Associates limited. Together with six partners, family and friends, Buffet raised $105,100 in capital. Buffet started two more partnerships. Buffet Fund Limited for which he had raised $120,000 and another limited partnership which had $55,000 in capital. Within the first year of trading, all three partnerships had made money.

*"in 1957 the three partnerships which we formed in 1956 did substantially better than the market.... All three of the 1956 partnerships showed a gain during the year amounting to about 6.2%, 7.8% and 25% on year end 1956 net worth."*[38]

Warren Buffet managed a number of partnerships for his family and friends. The partnerships outperformed the market during the early years and got him a lot of attention. By 1958, he had five partnerships in operation which returned between 36.7% and 46.2%[39]. Buffet's seventh partnership called Glenoff and consisting of $50,000 was established in 1959. Warren Buffet contributed $100 to each partnership and owed 9.5% of the combined partnerships. Over the next 13 years, the investments the partnerships made grew at a compounded annual rate of 29%. In 1965, when Buffett closed the partnerships, his combined share was $25 million. It was the management and actions in these years that laid the foundation for him as the greatest investor of all time. In nine years he multiplied his money many times over. From his life, we can see that investing and knowing how to invest multiplies your money.

# GOD, A MASTER INVESTOR

From the beginning we can see God as an investor. In Genesis 1, God plants two people on the earth and years latter his investment is now over 7 billion people. Even when these people fall, we see in John 3:16, God invested the life of his son Jesus Christ, that he might bring them back to be His. God sowed something by giving to the world and He reaped many times over and multiplied His returns. Out of one son, God gained hundreds of millions of sons. That is a good return for His investment! Jesus too taught a lot about investments in the New Testament. He gave various parables that illustrated investments, like the parable of the talents, where the master chastises the wicked servant because he hid his money and did not at least invest it with the bankers to get a small return. He gave the parable of the sower who scattered seed and some seeds did not give returns while others gave 30, 60 and 100 times returns. Jesus curses a fig tree because when he went to it, he did not find fruit (return) while he expected the tree to give a return to the world.

## MONEY MUST BE MULTIPLIED

We too have been put on the earth to be able to bear fruit and multiply the resources that have been given to us. Money is one of the resources that carry proof of our fruitfulness and multiplication. Money must be multiplied. An investment is anything that generates a return for the money put in. Investments are different from savings because investments make money work for you to provide you with a gain. Saving money is a good discipline. Saving alone however is not enough. Money that has been set aside through savings should be put to work. Money is a servant and must be made to work through multiplication.

In chapter 3, we looked at how you create a financial plan and setting of financial goals. Once you have your financial goals, these goals guide your investment decision. Recall the example of Jane Smith, her goal was to raise 300,000$ in investments that could generate 60,000$ each year that is 20% per annum in investment income. The investment horizon for Jane is 5 years and her target return is 30% per annum. Jane will have to look for and do due diligence on investment opportunities that can give her a 30% return per year for a period of at least 5 years. After 5 years, Jane will require an income from her investments. This will force her to get investments that can pay her some money, maybe yearly or even monthly. Just like Jane in this example the first step in determining an investment avenue is to know your goals, your investment horizon and how much you are targeting as interest or return per year.

# TYPES OF INVESTMENTS

There are various types of investments. Investments can be broadly categorized into short term that is less than one year, medium term 2 to 4 years and long term investments 5 years onwards depending on the likelihood of losing money or risks. Riskier investments will tend to be medium or long term investments. There are investments such as government bills and some cash funds that can be used for short term investing.

Investments would generally be categorized into the following.

1. Government Bills and Bonds

2. Shares Listed in a stock exchange

3. Real estate

4. Small businesses and start-ups

5. Private shares of companies

6. Collectables or precious metals

7. Other investments

Unit trust funds or Mutual funds are funds where a professional manager, usually an investment bank or insurance company pools the resources of different investors to put in different investment opportunities. The funds would usually be worth millions or billions of dollars and the professional manager charges a fee to invest in the fund. Thus, even a small investor can have access to these various investments through these funds.

These funds are classified from the most conservative to the most aggressive funds depending on where the money is invested.

# FUNDS CLASSIFICATION

**Money market funds:** The most conservative and the lowest earning of these funds is called the money market fund. In this fund, the manager will invest largely in cash or near cash investment options. This includes interest earning securities such as treasury bills and certificates of deposits. Some of the money may be invested in fixed interest bearing bank accounts. This fund provides low interest rate but the funds are largely accessible to the investor usually after a few days notice.

**Mixed funds:** The next type of fund is a mixed fund that will combine higher yielding investments such as stocks and low yielding ones such as bonds. This will be termed as a balanced fund because it seeks to balance between riskier investments and safer options such as bonds. As a result the return generated from these funds tends to be higher than the money market funds.

**Equity Funds:** The last broad category of funds will be aggressive funds that only invest in shares. These funds are the highest yielding funds of the three and over time tend to provide the best returns. In countries such as the United States and other countries across Europe and Asia listed stocks tend to be in the thousands. With this broad option it would take potential investors a lot of time and expertise to select the best investment options. For investors starting out, these funds are recommended because they provide diversification across different sectors. The funds may invest in different countries giving the investor access to high growth economies particularly in the emerging markets. Some funds limit their investments in a particular sector, region or stick to a particular strategy.

As you will notice in this chapter, we have not focused on the more traditional and common ways to invest. You still need to study these traditional investment types but I believe the best investments however are as a business owner. This may not necessarily include investing in the traditionally accepted investment avenues such as shares traded in a stock exchange. There are opportunities for investment all around us. What we require is to train our eyes to recognize them. The best investment avenue is your own calling or investing in the passion of others. Opportunities are more in developing countries as they have not yet maximized the potential of their countries. If your country has a lot of problems, investment opportunities are hidden in those problems. Begin to think, pray and get solutions to those problems and offer those solutions. You can partner also with people who have the solutions but may not have the money to start. However you have to educate yourself in business principles and develop in your area of calling.

## TYPES OF INVESTORS

It is not the type of investment or business that makes for a good investment. Many people ask me, is real estate a good investment? Is investing in hotels a good investment? Is investment in gas and oil sector a good investment? And so on. That is the wrong question to ask because the sector or area of business does not matter. Millionaires are being made today from work that did not exist 20 years ago. That means businesses are making money from opportunities that was not in existence 20 years ago. The critical question actually is, are you a good investor? Learning to invest is important. If you buy a house when it's overpriced and the market goes down and you are forced to sell for less, you have lost money and did not succeed at investing, even though the real estate market is booming. When you buy a house for less and you sell it at a profit, you have invested successfully.

## THERE ARE DIFFERENT TYPES OF INVESTORS

**1. Those who have nothing to invest.**

These categories of people are actually not investors. Unfortunately most people fall into this category. These are the people who spend all or more than they earn. They are the ones who end up poor when they stop working or end up trapped in debt. If you identify yourself in this category, it's important to note that this category is not permanent. Do something about it!

**2. Those who save.**

Saving is a very important discipline to learn. But there are those who only save money. They have money stashed somewhere in a bank account earning zero or near zero interest. Their savings stroke their egos and give them comfort. Like the rich man whose life was demanded from him, they want to be comfortable and enjoy their life. They hope to use this money for their retirement and feel safe because they have set aside money for the future. Even if you save 95% of your income, you're still losing money because of inflation. Each year, the prices of goods and services go up. Food prices have consistently gone up around the world over the last 100 years. The interest you receive from a bank is not enough to cover for the rate of increase in prices of goods and services. If you will require $100 in 10 years time to buy what you need $50 to buy today, you would have lost 50% of the value of your money in 10 years. If the bank pays you 3% for your savings and inflation is at 6% the value of your savings is wiped out. These investors lend their money to banks or other financial institutions, for which they receive a portion of the profit, but only a small percentage. The financial institution will take the bulk of the profit. The master in the parable of the sower admonishes the wicked and lazy servant, to have at least invested the talent with the bankers for some interest. At this level of investing, the returns expected are low but the money is accessible.

**3. Those who have others manage their investments.**

These are the people who not only manage to save but they turn their savings to '*experts*' to invest for them. They have limited financial education and they trust and invest their money in standard investments managed by investment banks and insurance companies. They mainly invest in mutual funds and the stock market. They are content to earn 10% per year. These also include those who seek to invest for themselves with little financial knowledge. They seek to buy real estate and handle the transactions themselves without seeking professional advice.

**4. Those who have mastered investing.**

These are the people who invest like business owners. They have increased their financial knowledge and take time to learn and master the principles of investing and the areas they are investing in. They surround themselves with skills and knowledge not only from their own learning but from the people they associate with. These investors do not necessarily use only their money to invest.

None of these levels are permanent and we all can fall in any of these categories. You determine where you operate from by your level of development. Several millionaires have been wiped out by business failures leaving them millions in debt. Even though it took them years, these men were still able to climb back out of debt, save, invest and make millions again. If you don't allow it, your situation is not fatal. Remember savings is for investment. You must learn the principles of investing and learn to track your investments. Invest as a business owner. Aim to develop yourself to the level of investing as a business owner using other people's money.

Gladys moved to the United Kingdom in 2004 after getting frustrated with the living conditions in her home country. She wanted a better life and once she got her Master's degree in Britain in 2008, she got a job earning better than an average income. For years, Gladys would spend all her money each month, from sending money to her parents back home to buying herself nice designer handbags and perfumes. Later she learnt to save and she would make some investments in the traditional avenues such as shares but she did not realize much growth. Once she understood that to achieve financial freedom she needed to do things differently, she got more aggressive in saving money, scaling down her lifestyle and living within 70% of her income. Within a year she was able to save $15,000 in 2014. She had identified a niche in her country. Middle income earners in her country of origin preferred European made cars to ones produced elsewhere. From her initial savings of $15,000 she bought and exported one car back home. She got a trusted friend to help handle import duty requirements and find market for the car. Out of that one car she was able to grow her investments to $23,000. She has continued to do this business and has streamlined her operation and now hires 5 sales people in her native country and exports at least 3 cars each month. Her initial capital has grown to over $100,000 over the last few years. She has used money borrowed from friends to buy more cars to send home particularly during peak holiday seasons but she is always able to pay back this money and still make profit from the sale of the cars. She is targeting to transition out of her job and concentrate on building her investments and her calling over the next two years with a capital of $300,000. She is working towards living within 50% of her income and investing all her business profits. Gladys grew from a type 1 investor, not saving anything to investing like a business owner, using other people's money to make money.

Aliko Dangote is Africa's richest man and the 51st wealthiest person in the world as at 2016. He is estimated to be worth around $12.9 billion dollars. He owns the Dangote Group which has interest in commodities and operates in several countries around the world. He developed an interest in business as a child, buying cartons of candies and selling them at a profit. In 1977, using capital provided to him by his grandfather, Dangote started to trade in commodities and building materials. Operating in a difficult manufacturing environment, with high costs and unstable electricity supply, he has built a vast empire consisting of food processing plants, telecommunications, steel, oil, gas and the main segment of the Group, the cement division. He describes in an interview how he used borrowed money to build the group's expansive cement plant in Obajana in central Nigeria, one of Africa's largest cement production plants. As global prices soared and demand for cement surged, he was able to repay a seven year loan within 18 months. He was able to multiply his investment many times over using other people's money. It is this Obajana Cement plant that propelled him into big business and prominence. Over the years his net assets have grown from $3.3 billion in 2007 to $22 billion in 2013, partly because of the success of his cement division in the Group.

## CONSIDER THIS WHEN PLANNING YOUR INVESTMENT

Before beginning an investment you need to plan and consider several things. This is to ensure that you are successful at the science of investing.

• **Willingness to take risk**

Investments and risk go together. There is a relationship between your potential return and the amount of risk you are willing to take. The risk described here is calculated risk. You need to take time to understand your investment and do due diligence on it. Know if you are willing to take the risk involved with the investment or not. Usually the benefits from such an undertaking would determine whether the investment is worthwhile or not. If an investment involves considerable risk while the return is low in comparison with similar investments, then it is not worth taking the risk.

### • Safety

When making an investment, you will have to factor in the probability of not receiving most or all your money back. If you want more guarantee of safety for your investment funds, you may have to take up safer investment options such as investment in money market funds. Usually such a decision would be taken if you need to use the money within a short time. For example in the period when you are accumulating your investment funds you may not want to take risk with the limited funds you have saved and so your investment options would be limited to fixed interest accounts and the like. You may also be accumulating your savings as startup capital for a business within a short term, usually a year or less. In this case then you may not be willing to make investments that do not guarantee a return of your funds. You cannot multiply your money however if you do not take some level of calculated risk.

### • Income

Some investment options provide regular income in form of dividends and interest. You need to determine how important receiving an income from your investment is and when you might want to do so. All this should form part of your financial plan. By the time you make investment decisions, you should know what you expect out of your investments. For example when you are still working and accumulating your savings and investments, you would want to focus on growing your investments hence you will not be looking for investments that will necessarily give you an income. This allows you the freedom to make investments in opportunities that can grow your money faster such as some real estate investments or business partnerships. Once you have hit your target financial goal, you can then convert some of your investments to generate an income for you. You can buy property to generate rental income or invest in stocks that provide good dividends. This would provide you with the passive income that allows you to still meet your financial obligations.

- **Growth**

At the initial stage the focus of your investment should be growth, unless your financial goal is to raise capital for business. In the initial months or years you should seek out opportunities that can grow your investment as quickly as possible. Let your target be to make investments that could generate returns of 30% per annum and above. However be careful to do due diligence and protect your investment using contracts or collateral.

- **Your time horizon**

The younger you are, the more time you have for your investments to grow. Typically, this means the more risk you may be willing to accept in exchange for the potential of higher returns. The older you are, the less time you have to weather the ups and downs of an investment. As a result, you may be more comfortable with predictable investments as opposed to more volatile, potentially higher growth opportunities.

- **Your financial position**

The more money and more your investments the more you are comfortable taking riskier investments.

Any potential loss is unlikely to be devastating to you financially. Since everyone has to start from somewhere, the less your net worth the more you need to invest time and energy into identifying good investment opportunities to grow your money. You will have to consider non-traditional types of investments, particularly small and medium size businesses. Most emerging new millionaires in America report having grown their wealth by investing in small businesses. Small and medium size businesses make up a significant part of the economy both in developed and developing world. Once you have acquired more money, then you are able to diversify some of your investments into more conservative ventures.

- **Your level of investment knowledge**

Generally, the higher your knowledge about investments, the more risk you may be willing to take. Professional investors such as Warren Buffet and other sophisticated investors are able to make above market returns because of their level of financial knowledge. Certain investment opportunities are only available to this level of investors. Make it your goal to grow your investment knowledge and experience to the level of sophisticated investors.

Before making any investments, it is critical within your financial plan to have an investment plan. The investment plan complements your overall financial plan and is meant to help you actualize your financial goals according to your set timelines.

# INSURANCE - TYPES OF INSURANCE

Typically, insurance is the way you will protect your gains. There are various types of insurance that help shield you against various possibilities in life. An insurance product should be carefully chosen after independent study on the various options in the market. Unfortunately the way most insurance companies choose to distribute insurance products is through sales agents who earn a commission on their sales. This presents a conflict of interest and the buyer must be careful not to take wholesome the advice dispensed by an agent with such conflict of interest.

We will review different types of insurance now:

## LIFE INSURANCE

A life insurance protects the future income of the insured against the possibility of death and disability over an agreed period. A life insurance policy does not protect against death, that's a certainty, neither does it provide life. The basic purpose of life insurance is to provide dependents with a source of income in case of death of the income earner. A life insurance contract pays the selected beneficiary an agreed lump sum or regular payments of cash to compensate them for the loss of the insured's income. Life insurance is paramount for married couples particularly those with dependants such as children. In the case of death of a spouse, the remaining spouse is left to shoulder the burden of raising children or providing for other dependants. The income generated by the deceased is no longer available. That can cause major strain on the finances of a family. It is therefore very important for married couples to discuss and protect both or one of their incomes in case of the death of either or both of them. It is important to ensure that the insurance cover is adequate enough to replace the lost income sufficiently. As a rule of thumb, make sure the insurance cover can pay off any outstanding loans, provide for future education and replace 10 years of your present income. Companies usually provide a life insurance cover as part of the employee benefits to their staff. The employee is responsible to find out how much cover the policy gives and whether it is sufficient to provide the family with replacement income. If it is adequate, there is no need to take up additional life insurance. Most times however, the insurance cover is not enough. It is better to have too much life insurance than to have insufficient life insurance.

For single people, depending on the responsibilities they shoulder, the effect of loss of income may not be as much. There are single people who have children or dependants such as parents or siblings. Those in this situation should take up life insurance to provide a replacement for their income in case of death. If however, a single person does not shoulder any such responsibilities it is an unnecessary expense to take up a life insurance cover.

It is important to note that a life insurance cover is not an investment and should not be taken as such. Insurance companies sometimes combine investment aspects to their life insurance products so that the premiums paid can be paid out at a later date to the owner of the life insurance policy. This sounds good in theory but comes at a price. The premiums charged for an insurance product that contains an investment option is usually many times more than a basic life cover. A basic life insurance product is called a term insurance and only pays out in case of the death of the insured. Some term insurance products may return the premiums paid by the insured at the end of the term and they are called value added term products. However the majority of term insurance products do not make any payments should the insured survive the insurance policy term period. They only pay in case of the death or disability of the insured. Term insurance products are usually the cheapest forms of insurance.

Other life insurance covers include a whole life insurance cover that provides an agreed sum of money in case of death or disability of the policy holders for the rest of their lives.

Endowment insurance provides insurance to the insured for a specific period of time during which the policy holder pays premiums. In case of death, the beneficiaries are paid the amount specified in the insurance contract. In case the insured survives the term of the contract, he will be paid the accumulated value of the insurance policy. This is usually a percentage above the total premiums contributed over the term. The yield on such a policy is usually low compared to investment in listed shares.

The cost of a whole life and an endowment insurance policy is much higher than the cost of a term insurance policy and the amount of cover you receive is usually lower. It is prudent to take basic term insurance only.

Given a scenario where a spouse takes up an endowment insurance policy of 30 years, the premiums say $3,600 per year or $300 per month may provide insurance cover for $200,000. At the end of the stipulated period the spouse may receive a lump sum payment of $200,000 having contributed a total of $108,000. In contrast a person who takes up a term insurance for the same period may end up paying $1000 per year for a life cover of $300,000. He will not receive any payment at the end of the contract, however if he invests the difference $2,600 over the 30 year period at 10% p.a, his investment would have grown to $470,453. Even after factoring in the loss of $1,000 per year, the latter ends up gaining more.

## DISABILITY INSURANCE

Most employers provide disability insurance for their employees in case of accident. Where one is in business, it is important to take up a disability cover. Sometimes a disability cover is lumped together with a life insurance cover or a medical insurance cover. Check the details of your insurance contract to ensure you have this cover. Disability insurance is designed to provide a payment to the insured in case of disability or loss of limbs due to an accident. The cover factors in the possible loss of income earning capacity due to disability.

## MEDICAL INSURANCE

Medical insurance pays for medical bills incurred by the insured person in case of hospitalization or during certain outpatient treatment. This will depend on the type of medical cover provided. In certain countries, the state provides health care benefits though they may not be adequate. It is important to study the contract to see what illnesses or medical procedures are excluded from such a cover. Again families should ensure the amount they are covered for is sufficient for medical emergencies that may arise. Medical bills can significantly dent your savings and investments. It is important to ensure you get a good comprehensive medical cover.

## MOTOR VEHICLE INSURANCE

This is insurance cover provided in case of theft or accident involving the insured motor vehicle. Depending on your country of residence, this is usually factored into the vehicle purchase payments particularly when taking up auto loans.

When buying any type of insurance, it is important to follow a few laws to ensure you get value for money. The first rule when buying insurance is to buy basic insurance. Insure only what would be financially disastrous if it occurred. If you can easily live without the product you are insuring then it's not worth insuring. Insurance against theft or loss of gadgets or clothing may fall within this category. The savings on the expense of insuring these items should go towards investments. From the investment income you can replace these items easily. However if you use certain items for work or business such as laptops, cameras and TV's it is important to ensure them to avoid loss of business as a result of loss or theft or damage to them. Remember insurance is meant to shield your investment gains not provide additional expenses.

In this chapter, we have covered several investment options from the traditional investments such as mutual funds, shares and bonds to investing as a business owner.

In summary the guidelines for investing at the end of this chapter are important to follow, they are keys to setting yourself free from the world system. In the next chapter, we will look at setting yourself free in more details.

# GUIDELINES FOR INVESTING

1. Don't look at your salary as an end in itself. Begin to look at your salary or income as a seed. Your salary is not the fruit to be eaten, it is a seed. If you are smart, you do not eat your seed. Seeds are meant to be planted. This does not refer to the popular doctrine of 'sowing seed' by giving to churches or pastors. Planting seeds refers to making good investment of your money.

2. Gather your income aside through savings. When savings are still small, you will need time to accumulate some amount of investable money. Take 30% to 50% of your income and work with it, in some business or trade or other investment so that it grows fast.

3. The best investment you can make is in yourself. In your skills and talents. You can use your savings to invest in buying equipment or tools for your profession or skill. Then begin to trade with the goods and services you produce to make money.

4. Any area of life can be a successful investment. You just need to have an understanding of the area where you have invested your money. You or the person you have invested in must be knowledgeable in the area and know how to do business in

that area. Invest in the right skilled people not so much the area of investment. Find out about the character of the people you invest in and whether they understand the laws of money.

5. Do your due diligence. Investigate the area of your possible investment as much as possible. If you are going into the business, know everything about the area. Find the people who are successful in that area and find out why. Find the principles of their success and interrogate them. If you are investing in other people find out their level of preparation and how much due diligence they have done.

6. Follow the Holy Spirit. Make sure you are led by the Spirit of God; go with what God tells you. If you are uncomfortable about a particular business, or have no peace about it, don't get into it. However do not be led by fear, the Spirit of God is not a spirit of fear. Do not allow for inaction in the name of waiting for God or under the guise of fear.

7. Take calculated risks. Have written legal and binding agreements with the people you are investing in, particularly in western countries where the court process is efficient. In some developing countries where this is not so, ensure you get collateral for your investment. When it comes to the court of law; if it is not written down, it does not exist. The conditions must be clearly spelled out and the document must be signed by both parties. Ensure you receive relevant legal advice.

8. Don't allow past failure in the area of invest-

ment to hold you back. You have to rise up from past failure; otherwise you can never be successful. Never stop attempting. The average millionaire in the United States has experienced bankruptcy at least once. Learn the lessons of failure and admit what you did wrong, investigate why you made the mistake and what you should do to prevent a repeat in the future.

9. Invest in people who have real products. They are either producing a good or a service. Do not invest in promises. Be wary of people not able to show you the product that is being transacted. Let people show you their track record, what they have done in the past.

10. Start out by investing in an amount of money that you can afford to live without. If you lose money, let go of the failures and learn the lessons of the failures and move to the next opportunity.

11. Build relationships in business. Take time to build trust and friendship with clients. Value people and relationships more than you value money.

12. Take interest in your investment. Any investment is investing your life. The money you are investing was gotten from the exchange of your time, therefore take it as seriously as you would your time.

13. Use insurance to protect your gains. Insurance products should only be used to provide replacement income in case of disability or death, to provide for healthcare or protect some of the

things you have in case of any loss. Insurance is not an investment and it should not be used as such.

# GOLDEN NUGGETS

- God planted two people on the earth and years later his investment is now over 7 billion people.

- Investments are different from savings because investments make money work for you to earn you a profit.

- Even a small investor can have access to these various investments through different types of funds.

- Millionaires are being made today from work that did not exist 20 years ago. That means businesses are making money from opportunities that were not in existence 20 years ago.

- You cannot multiply your money if you do not take some level of calculated risk.

- Once you have hit your target financial goal, you can then convert some of your investments to generate an income for you.

- Be careful to do due diligence and protect your investment using contracts or collateral.

- Make it your goal to grow your investment knowledge and experience to the level of sophisticated investors.

- The basic purpose of life insurance is to provide dependants with a source of income in case of death of the income earner.

CHAPTER 10

# SET YOURSELF FREE FROM THE WORLD SYSTEM

**"As sorrowful, yet always rejoicing; as poor, yet making many rich; as having nothing, and yet possessing all things."**

*(2 Corinthians 6:10)*

*The above scripture speaks of Apostle Paul's attitude in life. That when he was sorrowful he was still rejoicing, when he was poor, he was making others rich and when he had nothing he looked at himself as having all things. This is the same attitude we are to have if we are to be free from the world system.*

What would you do with the rest of your life if you inherited a million US Dollars? Take time to think about it. Most people would leave the job they currently have; even more would stop their businesses. Some would even leave the country they now reside in. That is the extent to which money determines our lives. We stay in jobs we would rather not do, we become discontent about our lives yet seem not to have power to do anything about it. If you have read this book up to this point, I have shared many principles that if you could apply them would change your life. The whole purpose of savings and subsequent investments is so that you can have the freedom to pursue your God-given vision and purpose.

## YOU CAN BE FREE – HOW TO OVERCOME THE WORLD SYSTEM

To overcome the world system, you must not subscribe to its values.

**First, you must not live your life for vanities and in pursuit of money.** Neither the world system nor anything in it; pride of life, lust of the eye and lust of the flesh must be found in you.

> **"I shall no longer speak many things with you, for the ruler of this world comes, and he has nothing in Me"**
>
> *(John 14:30)*

**Second, you must know the laws of money and stop serving money.** You need to master money, so as to use it to dominate and subdue the earth for God instead of serving money. Whatever is your motivation for work is your god. Money must not be your god, you must rule over money. Know how to manage money so that you can make money, direct money and make it work for you to get the things you want. It's no longer whether you have money or not that dictates what you can or cannot have. If you need to take your children to a particular school or own a particular house, once you have mastered money you know how to create it to get these things. Even though we will make money from our calling, our motivation is not the money but the desire to serve God.

The idea of work according to God's design is not survival but rather to fulfill purpose. Work is a means of fulfillment of purpose not for survival. In the Garden of Eden, Adam and Eve had everything they needed to survive. When they had not sinned, there was provision for everything they needed. Why did they still need to work?

**"And God blessed them. And God said to them, Be fruitful, and multiply and fill the earth, and subdue it. And have dominion over the fish of the sea and over the fowl of the heavens, and all animals that move upon the earth"**

*(Genesis 1:28)*

In Genesis 1:28, God gives them an assignment to work out. They were to be productive and fill the earth not just with children but with the products they were to create, the inventions they were to come up with. God expected them to build the earth just as heaven was and in building the earth they would subdue it. They were to rule in righteousness over the other creatures on the earth. Now dominion has taken a negative connotation to imply dictatorship and oppression without account-ability but that was not the intent. They were to have dominion on behalf of God, so they were to be stewards on the earth for God. The primary reason for their work was to serve God. From the beginning, God created work for our enjoyment and our fulfillment. Work is the way we are like God; He is a creator and so we also through work, we are creators and take pleasure through the things we create. Even God himself works. God is a creator through work and He takes pleasure in it. Work is not suffering, work is not a punishment and work is not a curse. Adam and Eve had not sinned by the time God gave them work. God took Adam to the Garden of Eden in Genesis Chapter 2 and told him to work; to keep and dress the garden. Work is one of the greatest blessings that God has given to humanity, for purpose and self- fulfillment. You need to discover what you were made to do, secure your financial future, pay yourself and set yourself free from the world system.

**Third, once you are no longer dependent on a job for survival, you still need to know what to do with your life.** For the majority of people even if they were given financial freedom, they would still not know what to do with their life. It is not just enough to be financially successful, you have to know what to do with it and with the freedom it affords you. You have to invest time to discover your purpose and begin to live it. Even as you do your job or daily occupation, begin to set aside time to explore who you are and what you were created to do. What do you like doing, what are you passionate about? What do you lose yourself in and forget the time? What do you find fulfillment and pleasure in doing? That could be an indicator of who you are supposed to be on earth.

The first purpose of work and employment is to bring the kingdom of God to rule in our work places.

**"But seek ye first the kingdom of God and his righteousness; and all these things shall be added unto you"**

*(Matthew 6:33)*

Your work should be to serve God. Work should be something Christians do to establish the will and purposes of God in their workplace not to pursue money. The sole purpose of work is to bring the virtues, righteousness, order and principles of God to our work places. Salaries and compensations are only rewards for our faithfulness in serving God not the motivation for work. Is your work a service to God?

**Forth, once you know your purpose, begin to enjoy work and find pleasure in it**. Even if you are not paid or you are paid little you can still enjoy what you do because you are not doing it for money but out of the pleasure of doing it. You still need to bargain for the best salary or compensation, but it's not your drive in doing your work. You may still need to work for a time in a place to raise money or to learn or as an apprentice, but you need to know why you are doing it and only for a short time. Set targets for yourself as to how much to set aside each month and how long you will work to raise the money needed, maybe 3 to 5 years. You still need to know other laws of money so that the world system does not swallow you.

I have told this story before in one my books. I was teaching my church workers in Kyiv some years back from the parable of the talents and God spoke to me and called me a wicked and lazy servant. When I asked Him why, he showed me that we were not even able to keep the money He had given us and we were running the church depending on income from each month without saving anything. I was worse than the wicked and lazy servant. At least he managed to save what the master had given him; I spend all that I was given each month without saving anything! From that point on I set out on a quest to know the laws of money and to master them. Over a year, as I studied further over that scripture and as I went out of my way to study more on the topic of wealth, I realized that every Christian could become a millionaire. I decided before I could teach my members on this I had to get results in my own life. I gave myself a target to become a millionaire within two years by mastering the laws of money. I was able to achieve that target within nine months. Recently when the Lord spoke to me to move to Nigeria, I was ready because I am financially free and I do not depend on the tithes and offerings of the church. I can risk leaving it all to follow my passion and calling. I challenge you to say the same.

Are you working for money? Do you hate your work? Take the decision to look for ways and means to set yourself free from the trap of the world system. Do everything you need to do to set yourself free from the slavery of the world system. Apply the principles outlined in this book and follow the examples of the people given here. Only note that you will not keep doing or living how you have been living, you may need to make painful life adjustments towards your goal. As you look at the strategies to set yourself free outlined below, approach them with the intention to implement them, first by taking time to meditate upon these steps, then applying them. As we conclude in the next chapter, I want to emphasize the purpose of money. It is said that when the purpose of a thing is unknown, the thing is bound to be misused. This is true of money especially in our day.

# STRATEGIES TO SET YOURSELF FREE

1. Perfect and develop your gifts and talents towards your calling. Then you can offer your service or product to other people. Even if you work for someone it will be on your own terms since you have developed yourself. When your passion and calling correspond with your skills, you are fulfilling God's purpose no matter who you work under.

2. The easiest way to set yourself free from the world is when your passion and purpose correspond to your work. Invest in building your business around your passion.

3. Pay yourself and set yourself free from the power of money. Work only to make and save enough money and then invest it. When your money works for you, you can then be free to pursue your calling.

4. Have too much money. If you have more than enough money, you are no longer tied to a job to survive. Less than 5% of the world has so much money that they do not need to work to survive.

5. Christians should only work with one purpose in mind; to bring the Kingdom of God into the sphere God is calling them to. To establish God's righteousness, virtues, principles and His order to that place of work. Ensure that you become financially free so you can boldly do this in your workplace without the fear of losing your job.

# GOLDEN NUGGETS

- Know how to manage money so that you can make money, direct money and make it work for you to get the things you want. It's no longer whether you have money or not that dictates what you can or cannot have.

- From the beginning, God created work for our enjoyment and our fulfillment. Work is the way we are like God.

- Even as you do your job or daily occupation, begin to set aside time to explore who you are and what you were created to do.

- Salaries and compensations are only rewards for our faithfulness in serving God not the motivation for work.

- You might still need to bargain for the best salary or compensation, but it's not your drive in doing your work

# CONCLUSION

# THE PURPOSE OF MONEY

**"For a man's life is not in the abundance of the things which he possesses"**

*(Luke 12:15)*

*The bible verse here is from a passage in which Jesus encountered a rich young man who is discontent. When he advised the young man to set himself free from the grip of money so that he could value what mattered, the young man was unable to follow Jesus and His advice. The same thing is happening to many people in the world today. They are unable to follow Jesus and to pursue His purpose for their lives because the pursuit or the ownership of money has preoccupied their lives. Money has become their Lord. That was not the original purpose of money. What then is the purpose of money?*

Money is a creation of Man. From the Old Testament, men began from barter exchange; exchanging goods for goods. Livestock was bartered in exchange for farm produce, and then developed when goods were exchanged for spices and precious metal. With time men developed the system of money, then a form of precious metal, such as silver. We see Abraham buying a piece of land with money in Genesis 23:13. Money was used as a tool to make the trade easier. When they could not exchange livestock for farm produce anymore, the people moved to exchange livestock for precious metal. They then realized that they needed to make the exchange fair so that one party did not give more than the product's worth or the other party did not get less than the product's worth. So they introduced a system of weighing precious metal in exchange for a product and a system of pricing a product. So when Abraham bought the land he actually weighed some quantity of silver to the seller. What was considered more precious cost more weight in silver than what wasn't as valuable. During the time of Isaac they introduced a standard unit of weight as a shekel. A shekel was 8.4 grams of silver. This weight was counted as money. There were shekels of gold, of silver and of barley. When Abraham's servant went to get a wife for Isaac in Genesis 24, he gave her gifts in the form of shekels. Money continued to evolve over the ages. Coins were introduced in Asia Minor by the merchants there who wanted to avoid weighing them each time they traded. They put a stamp with the official seal on the coins to certify their weight. By the time Jesus was on earth, Roman coins bore the face of the ruler of the Roman Empire, Caesar. Money, as you can see is a recent invention.

### 1. Money is an answer and a defense

The shift from the Agrarian system to the industrial age and now the technological age means money now is essential for life. Before you could grow your food, build on the land and live without money. The book of Ecclesiastes tells us that money has the properties to answer to all things and it is a defense[42]. These properties of money cause many people to put their trust in money. They begin to see money as all they need and they prioritize money above everything else. At this point they are worshiping money.

### 2. Money is not to be worshipped

There is a spirit behind the money that seeks to be worshiped, mammon. As Christians the Bible warns us not to trust in riches even when we have them.

> **"Charge them that are rich in this world, that they be not high-minded, nor trust in uncertain riches, but in the living God, who gives us richly all things to enjoy"**
>
> *(1Timothy 6:17)*

### 3. Money does not give identity

> **"He who trusts in his riches shall fall"**
>
> *(Proverbs 11:28)*

Riches can be deceitful. Scripture describes riches as being deceitful, and in trusting money we become deceived. If we hope to get our identity or our fulfillment and satisfaction from money, we have been deceived. Money does not give identity. Money doesn't give joy and fulfillment and money does not give purpose to man. If we do not understand that we are deceived. If money defines who we are, whether we are happy or not, we are deceived. When we look to money to do the things only God can do, we begin to worship money and it becomes our master. Money is a terrible master; it corrupts us and only causes us to become trapped in the world system. Our hope, our shield, our trust is not in money but in

God. He is the one who gives us these things for our enjoyment. We cannot master money unless we understand this.

# EXAMINE YOUR MOTIVES

You have read this book to learn how to secure your financial future and enjoy financial freedom. What is your motivation to become rich in money? What is the goal for the money you want to get? If money does not serve the purpose of advancing the kingdom of God, that money will enslave its owners. If money is only for yourself; to make your life comfortable, to give you esteem and status, to please your family only, it will end up entrapping you. Jesus encountered the rich young ruler in Mathew 19:16 and despite his wealth, he was still looking for something more. And Jesus upon interacting with him realized that he was entrapped by money. To deliver him, Jesus told him in verse 21 to sell all that he had and follow Him. The young man was not able to obey because the riches had him. He loved the lifestyle his possessions could afford him more than he loved God and he therefore missed more than he was searching for. The wealth was serving him, it was his identity, it was for his ego and he couldn't let go. This doesn't mean that Christians should not have possessions or that we should all sell what we have; Jesus was trying to deliver the man from what had already entrapped him. But we are to ensure that our possessions do not entrap us in the first place. We are to live as though we have nothing, yet possessing all things.

Money is for advancing the Kingdom of God. Our motives for desiring money must be pure. Your agenda must be for the advancement of the kingdom of God and not to earn a living or to survive. You will never have enough for yourself when your mentality is to survive or make ends meet. You barely make enough when your goal is too small, only you and your family. You will be content with too little. If you got a million dollars or even a billion dollars for you and your family you would easily be content. However when your goal is to end world poverty, for example, even a billion dollars is too little for your vision. You must desire to have money to pursue your God-given vision, to advance the agenda of God on the earth. When you do that, because of the size of your vision, your energy increases and doors open for you to larger amounts of money than you would have had if you only focused on yourself and your family. Imagine if Henry Ford had focused on only building cars for himself and his family. He could only have produced a few cars, no one would know him. The world would not be remembering him almost a hundred years later. Henry Ford became wealthy and the generations of his family after him because he had a big vision; he dreamt of producing cars for the world.

When you are living for something greater than you, then you are successful. When you work for the kingdom of God and its larger good, it always benefits you. Make up your mind that the only thing you are living for and working for is God and His Kingdom.

Use money for the purpose of subduing your area of calling for God. Each one of us has a particular sphere where we are called to bring the values and virtues of God, God's order, His righteousness and His principles into. The Bible shows us that we have all been reconciled to God and we have been given the ministry of reconciliation.[43]

Money meets needs. Once we know the laws of money and we master money, we can direct it on how and where to go, what needs to meet and what causes to accomplish. We are not to follow the dictates of money, we direct money where to go and what to do. To do this we must conquer money, first by overcoming our own greed, lust of the eye, lust of the flesh and the pride of life. We must deal with our emotions, our desires, our passions, our ego and the urge to show off. Regulate and control your wants, wishes, appetite and tastes. When you receive money and are not immediately driven to spend it, then you can direct money.

It is important to remember when dealing with money, that money is created to serve us. We were not created to serve money; we were created to serve God. God and God alone is the one we love and live for with our all. Having a proper and correct value system sets us free from the enslavement of money and the deceitfulness of riches; money ceases to run you. Our drive becomes serving God and His people; our agenda becomes to fulfill our purpose and thereby advancing the Kingdom of God on the earth.

Make money your slave. Use money to advance the kingdom of God by fulfilling your purpose, to free you to focus on your call. Build your secured financial future.

# REFERENCES

**The trap of the world system**

1. High Income improves evaluation of life but not emotional well- being by Princeton's Daniel Kahneman & Angus Deaton

2. BRIC- Brazil, Russia, India, China

3. Webster's Dictionary

4. Bible, 2 Corinthians 4:4

5. Bible, 1 John 2:16

6. Bible, Mark10:17

7. Bible, Mathew 7:26

8. According to Transparency International

9. Organization for Economic Co-operation & Development, OECD data 2014

10. Bible, Romans 6:16

11. Bible, Revelations 11:15

12. Bible, Mark 12:30

13. Bible, John 5:19

14. Bible, Malachi 2:15

**Importance of paying yourself**

15. International Labor Organization 2015 data

16. Bible, Psalms 3:3 & Genesis 15:1

17. NBA-National Basketball Association

18. Sports Illustrated 2009 article, How and Why Athletes go broke

19. Bible, Genesis 28:22

20. Bible, Luke 16:13

**The discipline of saving**

21. Source ABCNews.com

22. Strive Masiyiwa Official Facebook Page

23. Gross Domestic Product, A measure of the income produced in a country

24. Old Mutual Wealth Savings & Investment Monitor Survey 2015

25. World bank Global Savings data

**How the rich use money**

26. Statistics taken from Thomas Corley's book Rich Habits

27. Bible, Mathew 19:21

**Control your appetite**

28. Bible, 1 John 2:16

29. Webster's dictionary definition

30. Bible, Romans 12:2

31. Bible, Mathew 4:1-11

32. Bible, Mathew 6:33

**Build your future**

33. Reuters

34. From the documentary Crocodile in the Yangtze

35. Strive Masiyiwa Official Facebook page

36. Strive Masiyiwa official Facebook page

37. From the book Teacher man by Frank McCourt

**Investments**

38. Warren Buffet Annual letter to limited partners 1957

39. Warren Buffet Annual letter to limited partners 1958

40. Forbes World's Billionaires list 2016

41. Financial Times article 2013, Aliko Dangote-Africa's Richest Man

**Conclusion; the purpose of money**

42. Bible, Ecclesiastes 7:12

43. Bible, 2 Corinthians 5:18

# Sunday Adelaja Bio

Sunday Adelaja is a Nigerian born Leader, Transformation Strategist, Pastor, and Innovator.

At 19, he won a scholarship to study in the former Soviet Union. He completed his master's program in Belorussia State University with distinction in journalism.

At 33, he had built the largest evangelical church in Europe; The Embassy of the Blessed Kingdom of God for All Nations.

Sunday Adelaja is one of the few individuals in our world who has been privileged to speak in the United Nations, Israeli Parliament, Japanese Parliament, and United States Senate.

The movement he pioneered has been instrumental in reshaping lives of people in the Ukraine, Russia and about 50 other nations where he has his branches.

His congregation, which consists of ninety-nine percent white Europeans, is a cross-cultural model of the church for the 21st century.

His life mission is to advance the Kingdom of God on earth by raising a generation of history makers who will live for a cause larger, bigger, and greater than themselves. Those who will live like Jesus and transform every sphere of the society in every nation as a model of the Kingdom of God on earth.

His economic empowerment program has succeeded in raising over 200 millionaires in the short period of three years.

Sunday Adelaja is the author of over 300 books; many of which are translated into several languages including Russian, English, French, Chinese, German, etc.

His work has been widely reported by world media outlets such as; The Washington Post, The Wall Street Journal, New York Times, Forbes, Associated Press, Reuters, CNN, BBC, German, Dutch and French national television stations.

Pastor Sunday is happily married to his "Princess" Bose Dere Adelaja. They are blessed with three children; Perez, Zoe and Pearl.

# FOLLOW SUNDAY ADELAJA
## ON SOCIAL MEDIA

**Subscribe And Read Pastor Sunday's Blog:**

www.sundayadelajablog.com

**Follow These Links And Listen To Over 200 Of Pastor Sunday's Messages Free Of Charge:**

http://sundayadelajablog.com/content/

**Follow Pastor Sunday on Twitter:**

www.twitter.com/official_pastor

**Join Pastor Sunday's Facebook page to stay in touch:**

www.facebook.com/pastor.sunday.adelaja

**Visit our websites for more information about Pastor Sunday's ministry:**

http://www.godembassy.com
http://www.pastorsunday.com
http://sundayadelaja.de

# Contact

For distribution or to order bulk copies of this book, please contact us:

**USA**
CORNERSTONE PUBLISHING
info@thecornerstonepublishers.com
+1 (516) 547-4999
www.thecornerstonepublishers.com

**AFRICA**
Sunday Adelaja Media Ltd.
Email: btawolana@hotmail.com
+2348187518530, +2348097721451,
+2348034093699.

**LONDON, UK**
Pastor Abraham Great
abrahamagreat@gmail.com
+447711399828, +44-1908538141

**KIEV, UKRAINE**
pa@godembassy.org
Mobile: +380674401958

# BEST SELLING BOOKS BY DR. SUNDAY ADELAJA

The Kingdom Driven Life:
Thy Kingdom Come, Thy
Will be Done on Earth
(Best seller)

Myles Munroe:
... Finding Answers To Why Good
People Die Tragic And Early Deaths

Nigeria And
The Leadership Question:
Proffering Solutions To Nigeria's Leadership Problem

Olorunwa (There Is Sunday):
Portrait Of Sunday Adelaja.
The Roads Of Life.

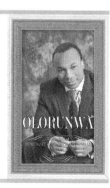

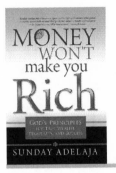

Money Won't Make You Rich:
God's Principles for True
Wealth, Prosperity, and Success

Who Am I? Why Am I here?:
How to discover your
purpose and calling in life

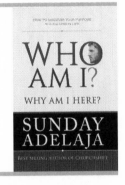

Only God Can Save Nigeria:
What a Myth?

Church Shift:
Revolutionizing Your Faith, Church,
and Life for the 21st Century

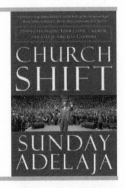

... and many more.

Made in the USA
Middletown, DE
08 June 2023

32250148R00137